HIKE BEYOND PAYCHECK

Saurav Pal

Clever Fox
PUBLISHING

Chennai • Bangalore

CLEVER FOX PUBLISHING
Chennai, India

Published by CLEVER FOX PUBLISHING 2023
Copyright © Saurav Pal 2023

CONTENTS

Dedication

This book is dedicated to parents, wife and all of my community members who are taking actions & producing bigger results in their journey.

Thanks for trusting me & making me whoever I am today.

ABOUT THE AUTHOR

Saurav Pal

Saurav Pal, is a visionary entrepreneur, content creator & a mentor. He took a life-changing decision in 2019 that got him on the journey to impact millions of corporate professionals across the country. He left a prestigious position in Dubai behind, with unshakeable faith to begin on a journey of empowerment and professional growth.

Presently, Saurav Pal is leading one of the largest communities of working professionals in india, catering to both IT and non-IT sectors. His transformative workshops have empowered over 150,000 individuals, solidifying his reputation as a prominent National Figure in the field of professional development.

Saurav's training program owns an impressive enrollment of nearly **10,000** active members. The best part is, he does not focus on conventional ways/knowledge, rather shares his deeper insights and proven methodologies derived from his remarkable global exposure & this is evident in the results of his mentees.

His story, began with a small monthly wage of **10,552/-** but he refused to continue longer with that mediocrity. <u>Within just the</u>

<u>first three years</u> of his job, Saurav defied the odds and surpassed multiple barriers to reach a monthly salary equivalent to **27 times** of his 1st salary. His simple yet effective motto is to *"Observe, Adapt, and Implement as quick as possible"*

As part of his mentorship programmes, Saurav imparts his hard-won knowledge, enabling participants to strategically launch their careers and get many job offers within a few months of diligent preparation. Thanks to his step-by-step teaching, thousands of learners from his community have experienced astonishing pay raise ranging from **80% to 600% jump.**

Moreover his mentees are also successfully acing the interviews and landing high-profile jobs in countries like Dubai, Abu Dhabi, Vietnam, London, and the USA.

Saurav concentrates on important topics including interview tactics, salary negotiation skills, handling HR objections, profile optimisation, LinkedIn & naukri profile ranking, and much more. He has been invited on the **National Television** Channel (Economics Times) for his exceptional work & sharing his wisdom. He is moving forward with a goal of empowering 10 million lives to skyrocket their income, life & success.

Saurav has transformed the learning environment for working people as the creator of the very acclaimed "**Massive Hike Formula**." His professional-focused, results-driven programme carefully trains participants to get high-paying job offers. The Massive Hike Formula helps individuals to improve their employability, raise their income, gain respect, and explore worldwide opportunities through step by step training courses **+** live interactive sessions by Saurav himself.

> **"You are bound to make it big. Take on the challenges, seize the opportunities, and forge your own path to an extraordinary journey."**

Connect with Saurav Pal at:

www.sauravpal.com

Instagram | Youtube | Linkedin : @sauravpalclub

BOOk INTRODUCTION

Dear Amazing Reader,

This book is not suitable for you, if you are satisfied with a mediocre life or if you have no interest in adding a spark to your career. It contains —**no theoretical gyan or empty promises**. Instead, it offers practical insights that provide a fresh perspective on life, career, and professional growth.

However, if you treat this book as just another addition to your bookshelf, it will be meaningless and serve no purpose. Even if you read just one page a day, it signifies progress in your journey.

I understand that reading a book can be uncomfortable, just as writing a book, preparing for interviews, changing your environment is uncomfortable. Infact making progress can be uncomfortable. But does that mean, that you would not take actions for your growth? No right…

You are starting a new life with this book, pay attention and be willing to embrace the change. This book reflect my thoughts and actions that helped to accelerate my career in India and abroad. It contains fail-proof strategies and real-life scenarios that I and thousands of my mentees have implemented to accelerate their careers. Ignoring this book and its practical insights would be a missed opportunity.

Even today, a lot of talented people like you, are trapped with education loans, heavy EMI's and are unable to attain their full potential in their careers & life. The youth face numerous challenges and problems.

Hence, It is important to raise awareness and learn how to tackle these situations effectively. That's why we have kept the content of this book, easy to understand & included examples at certain places for better relatability. This is a must-read for you.

With every chapter you go-through, you will gain confidence, feel empowered, learn new tactics and be inspired to take actions in your journey. I encourage you to dive into it and discover a new version of yourself. This is how i want to contribute in your life & when you get the **power bombs** while reading this book, do gift a copy to someone you really care for. Let's add value & contribute in as many lives possible.

Stay amazing, stay focused, and stay grounded on your journey.

Let's begin the path of Practicality.

PRAISE

I met Saurav Pal for the very first time in August 2019 when he had come to attend one event in New Delhi.

He had specifically traveled all the way from Dubai so that he can learn from that event. This showed his dedication and focus towards growth and excellence.

In the last 4 years he has helped thousands of working professionals excel in their fields and get a hike in their respective careers.

His work has indeed been noteworthy; not only has he generated revenue for himself but he has guided individuals grow through his expertise & has created employment for a lot of people. Many congratulations Saurav for your book.

I am 100% sure that this book will empower lakhs of people and help them become more able & highly skilled to do so much more in their lives.

Rahul Bhatnagar

Content Creator | Educator | Best Selling Author ~ Rise & Shine

Saurav is not just a traditional career coach rather he is empowering thousands of people with massive salary hike in his unique way. I know him for past 2 years & has seen his results & growth.

This book will serve as an Ultimate Guide for someone, who want to accelerate in their professional journey. Most of your mis-beliefs, doubts & concerns will be resolved with every progressive chapter you go through.

Read it and most importantly, implement the learnings. You will love it.

Siddharth Rajsekar

Founder-Internet Lifestyle Hub |Best Selling Author - You can Coach

ACKNOWLEDGEMENTS

This book has been possible with the outstanding efforts of various people.

I have been thinking of writing a book since a long time but the only reason there was no progress because I thought I'll do it all on my own. But later I realised, we need to divide the roles & keep practical deadlines for every job task.

I'll start with Ashima, my wife with whom I started planning topics & content to be included in the book. She took this book publishing project, more seriously than me :D

Later, Akash who looks our operation & delivery also got involved in ideation & processes.

Coordination for the book structuring was overlooked by Gulshan, Nishita and kudos to Alok, for patiently doing various changes in the book cover design.

To the cleverfox team for their support in the overall process.

I am forever grateful to few special people, their inputs in my journey have been valuable. [Rahul & Saurabh Bhatnagar,

Siddharth Rajsekar, Himanshu Agrawal & Purushottam Hambarde, Abhishek Pal]

I would also like to appreciate some of our community members, who have shared their journey/experience in this book to inspire the readers on a deeper level. [Mohini, Lekha, Naresh, Jitendra, Priyanka, Justin, Bhanu, Sowjanya, Tejomay, Nikhil, Monalisa Sahil Goura] & many others.

And finally a big shout out to all of my Team-Mates/FamilyMembers/ Cousins/ in-laws. The love, respect & appreciation that they all showed throughout this journey has been irreplaceable.

Chapter 1

WHY DO YOU NEED A RAISE?

How a Raise Can Boost Employee Morale

> *"True success embraces the entire journey with a spirit of gratitude; it encompasses more than reaching a destination."*

In the field of employee satisfaction, motivation and appreciation are more than simply trendy buzzwords; they are vital pillars that determine the nature of a meaningful and stimulating work environment. We begin a fascinating investigation of how a raise can act as a potent catalyst, changing the dynamics within an organization.

In the first chapter, get ready to see the extraordinary effect a raise can have on employee as we explore the complex relationships between the quest for excellence, receiving recognition, growth and job satisfaction.

INCREASED MOTIVATION: IGNITING THE FLAME WITHIN.

One of the primary advantages of a raise lies in its ability to ignite a powerful flame of motivation within employees. When an individual receives a raise, it goes beyond a mere financial increase. This recognition and appreciation nurtures their intent and cultivates a sense of fulfilment.

A raise catalyzes self-belief and confidence. It provides employees with a renewed sense of purpose, empowering them to take ownership of their work and strive for even greater success. With the recognition that their efforts are acknowledged and rewarded, employees are inspired to maintain their high level of performance and continuously improve their skills and expertise.

Furthermore, a raise signifies not only financial growth but also personal and professional growth. It communicates to employees that their potential is recognized and that there are opportunities for advancement within the organization. This acknowledgement and encouragement create a positive feedback loop, where employees are driven to excel and contribute their best to the success of the company.

HOW A RAISE CAN IMPACT YOUR PERSONAL + PROFESSIONAL LIFE:

"Unleash the Power of a Raise: Uplifting Growth, Stability, and Fulfillment Beyond the Workplace"

Beyond its immediate impact on salary, a raise corresponds throughout an employee's personal life, bringing about transformative changes that extend far beyond the workplace. A raise holds the potential to shape an individual's personal + professional life in numerous ways, ranging from (career growth & financial well-being) to (overall happiness and fulfilment).

With a higher income, employees experience a sense of relief from the stress and worries associated with their finances & family. This newfound stability empowers them to take control of their situation, effectively manage their expenses, and plan for the future.

They can now afford to invest in their well-being, such as engaging in activities that promote health and wellness, and pursue personal interests and hobbies that were previously out of reach. This improved financial stability positively influences various aspects of their personal life, leading to a more fulfilling and balanced existence.

DOES UNCERTAINTY & RISK ASSOCIATED WITH HIGH PAY.

> *"No uncertainty, No risk. Hardly 1% of people comes to a compromising situation, and even if it happen, it's an opportunity rather."*

Life is an unpredictable adventure, and our working lives are no different. Though it is always with us, uncertainty is nothing to be dreaded. In reality, it frequently serves as a catalyst for opportunity and advancement. Even though extreme situations, like losing your job, are uncommon, they sometimes offer hidden opportunities. We are never aware what god has in plan for us in the near future.

HIGH PAY DOES NOT BRING HIGH RISK.

A great salary does not always translate to great risk. It's critical to change the way we think about risk and realise that it's not just a function of our paycheque. Instead, it has to do with our capacity to significantly improve the company. Risk largely affects those who aren't contributing enough towards the project/client/ organisation during tough scenarios like pandemics and recessions.

When faced with uncertainty, we must welcome the unexpected and see it as a platform for both personal and professional growth. We have the option to view uncertainty as an opportunity to reach previously unachievable heights rather than letting fear hold us back.

Let's not forget that our capacity to adapt, think creatively, and make a positive difference also determines risk. We can successfully navigate unpredictable times by concentrating on providing value and being strong in the face of difficulty. As a result, we will be stronger and more prosperous than ever.

Whenever you have multiple doubts. Think about these 2 choices:

a. Will you keep thinking about the 1% risk & not step forward for your massive results & growth.

b. Or you will prove your worth to the organisation and claim the higher gains possible.

YOUR WORTH IS MUCH HIGHER THAN THE RAISE YOU ARE LOOKING FOR!

> *"We often undervalue ourselves but the truth is, you are worth much more than your current compensation package."*

It's crucial to understand that our value goes much beyond monetary evaluations. The money we make, just scratches the surface of our genuine potential. Instead of giving in to greed or materialistic wants, it's important to recognise the enormous worth that each of us brings to the table.

You tell me, don't you feel that you will deliver the best value to your project/company/client for the amount of CTC that you are demanding for? You will right..!! The time, energy, skills, experience & knowledge that you will put in that project is worth of the **raise** that you are looking for.

There is a clear link between your own growth and the happiness of the people closest to us. When we accept this profound connection, a universe of limitless opportunities becomes possible. By accepting our genuine value, we give ourselves the freedom to explore new possibilities, enlarge our horizons, and improve both our own lives and the lives of others.

So, give up self-doubt and accept your genuine worth. Recognise your special abilities, life experiences, and point of view. You allow yourself and the people you care about access to incredible growth, fulfilment, and success by doing so.

LEARNING CURVE + FINANCIAL CURVE

"Some people say you should focus only on learning, but I beg to differ!"

In the pursuit of personal and professional growth, the debate between prioritizing learning or focusing solely on financial success is a common one. While some argue for education as the primary focus, I believe in striking a balance between continuous learning and financial development. Both aspects are crucial in building a successful and fulfilling career.

The learning curve represents the ongoing process of acquiring new skills, expanding knowledge, and developing expertise in a field. It is essential for staying relevant, adapting to change, and seizing new opportunities in today's fast-paced world. By investing in your learning curve, you ensure competitiveness and adaptability.

Equally important is recognizing the value of financial growth and stability. Financial development provides the resources and opportunities to leverage skills effectively. It enables taking on new challenges, exploring diverse avenues, and pursuing passions without financial constraints. Nurturing both the learning and financial curves creates a harmonious balance that propels individuals towards success.

When the learning curve and financial growth go hand in hand, a synergistic effect occurs. Investing in learning enhances market value, opening doors for financial advancement. Monetizing expertise and knowledge lead to higher salaries, promotions, and entrepreneurial endeavours.

Moreover, prioritizing both learning and financial development demonstrates self-worth and confidence. It sends a message that expertise and contributions are valuable, fostering a positive career trajectory. By seeking growth opportunities and recognizing the importance of fair compensation, individuals empower themselves on their journey to success.

RIPPLE EFFECT ON FAMILY: SHARING THE REWARDS TOGETHER

"Your success and happiness matter to your loved ones. Share the rewards with those who sacrificed for you."

Throughout your journey, your parents and other family members have been a constant source of support and encouragement. They have selflessly put aside their own goals and aspirations to provide you with a better life and opportunities. Now, as you begin to achieve success and financial stability, it's an opportunity to give back and share the rewards with those who have sacrificed for you.

"Infact what I feel is, your parents & loved ones wait for your success unconditionally."

As you start to make a good living, it's essential to remember the profound impact your achievements can have on your family. It's not merely about accumulating wealth for yourself, but also about using some of it to create special memories and fulfill the aspirations of your loved ones. Let them know how much their support has meant to you.

One way to share the rewards is by treating your family to experiences they may have never dreamed possible. Plan vacations or outings that allow you to bond and create lasting memories together. Whether it's a trip to a dream destination, a special celebration, or simply spending quality time together, these experiences will serve as a reminder of your gratitude and appreciation for their sacrifices.

Additionally, consider supporting your loved ones in realizing their own aspirations. Your success can open doors for them and provide opportunities to pursue their passions or dreams. Whether it's funding their education, helping them start a business, or supporting their personal goals, your financial stability can be a catalyst for their growth and fulfillment.

Remember, success is not solely measured by individual accomplishments but rather by the positive impact we have on the lives of those we care about. So, as you embark on this journey of success, carry with you the understanding that your achievements have the power to create a ripple effect of joy, fulfillment, and gratitude within your family.

KEY TAKEAWAYS:

- Accept uncertainty as a chance for development and discovery because the likelihood of being asked to leave is quite low.
- Realise that you are worth more than the numbers on your paycheck and that your contributions to your company are priceless.
- Maintain a healthy balance between your learning and money curves, keeping in mind that both are necessary for both personal and professional fulfilment.
- A pay rise serves as a kind of appreciation and recognition that motivates you to work harder and do more.
- Share your accomplishments and rewards with the people you care about most so that you might grant their wishes and fulfil their ambitions.

To summarise, a big boost provides more than just a pay rise. It offers chances for development, self-discovery, and the opportunity to thank and assist those who have supported you. Unleash your potential for an incredible and gratifying experience by harnessing the power of a wild walk.

HOW TO FIND THE RIGHT JOB?

Unlocking the Path to Your Dream Job.

> *"Your dream job is waiting to be discovered. Let's embark on a journey to find it together."*

It is imperative to arm yourself with the appropriate ideas and approaches to traverse the constantly changing environment in today's fiercely competitive job market, where the search for the ideal opportunity can frequently feel like a difficult expedition. A well-crafted strategy is necessary to land a job that not only aligns with your talents but also with your hobbies and career goals. We'll go out on a quest to learn the keys to opening the doors to your ideal career in this chapter.

Because the job search process can be intimidating, we will explore in detail the procedures and strategies that can greatly increase your chances of success. We will arm you with the knowledge and resources required to competently navigate the competitive job market, from optimising your web profile and fine-tuning your resume to utilising the power of networking and preparing for interviews.

1: USING THE POTENTIAL OF ONLINE JOB PORTALS:

> *"Unleash the Power of Job Search Websites: Your Gateway to Career Success!"*

Starting a job hunt may be both thrilling and intimidating. Thankfully, the internet has transformed how we look for work, and job search websites have become crucial resources as a result.

Let's explore these websites and see how they can assist you in obtaining your ideal position.

Indeed, the Job Giant:

As one of the biggest job search websites, Indeed commands attention with millions of job ads from across the globe. Make use of its robust search tools to locate pertinent job vacancies by keyword, geography, employer, or job type. Even better, you can use the site to directly apply while uploading your profile. With job alerts that let you know when the ideal opportunity matches your interests, you can stay ahead of the game.

LinkedIn, the Professional Powerhouse:

For job hunters, LinkedIn is one of the premium platforms. Create a great profile that highlights your qualifications and use the platform to look for work, communicate with recruiters and hiring managers, and join organisations for your field to take advantage of networking opportunities. Receive job alerts that are customised to your abilities and experience to keep you informed of any new possibilities.

Glassdoor, the Insider's Guide:

With Glassdoor, you can unleash the potential of company reviews, pay data, and interview advice. This priceless tool equips you with crucial knowledge to make wise judgements and ace job interviews as you study possible employers. You may easily submit applications on Glassdoor and search for jobs using a variety of parameters, just like on other platforms.

There are various other platforms that you can use in your journey:

- Naukri
- Careerbuilder
- Monster
- And many other…

Fast-track Your Job Search:

Keep the following advice in mind to maximise your success on job-hunting websites:

- **Make your application materials unique:** Create your CV specifically for each job to show that you are interested in the position and are a good fit. <u>Don't use a common profile to apply for every job.</u> For each job application, modify your resume to reflect the right balance between you & the role of the position.

- **Create Job Alerts:** Make use of the tools that let you know when new positions that meet your criteria become available by sending you the job notifications. This will save you time and effort.

- **Craft your Video Resume:** This will simply boost your interview calls to atleast **4X**.

(More details about video resume is shared in an upcoming chapter)

- **Be Proactive:** Don't wait for chances to come to you. Contact the businesses that interest you and enquire about any prospective job openings.

You'll set yourself up for success in your job search by utilising job search websites wisely and taking a proactive stance. Prepare to open new doors and get hold of the career of your dreams.

2: PROFILE OPTIMIZATION:

"Your profile is your digital introduction to the professional world."

Your online presence acts as your digital debut to the professional world in the current era. Making a good first impression and optimising your profile is essential given that prospective employers frequently use websites like LinkedIn to look for applicants. Here's how to improve your profile and raise your chances of getting the job of your dreams:

Update and review your profiles regularly:

Examine your present online profiles on sites like Meta, Twitter, and LinkedIn to start. Make sure they are correct and reflect your education, talents, and professional experience. Remove any information that is out-of-date or unrelated. Create a captivating headline or summary that highlights your candidature and career goals, and use a professional & recent profile photo.

Highlight Your Experience and Skills:

Putting your relevant experience and talents on display is a crucial part of optimising your web presence. To make yourself more discoverable to employers, use sector-specific keywords and phrases. List your achievements in bullet points and emphasise the influence you had in past employment. Demonstrate your knowledge and abilities.

Ensure Your Online Presence Is Professional:

Even on personal social media accounts, it's critical to maintain a professional presence. Sharing stuff that is offensive or controversial damages your reputation. Use privacy settings to limit who can see your posts, and take care of the information you publish online. Keep in mind that while considering you for a job, potential employers may look at your social media sites.

3: RIGOROUS FOLLOW-UPS:

"Persistence is the key to unlocking opportunities."

We emphasised the value of networking in your job hunt in our previous content. However, networking isn't enough by itself to land a job. Following up with your existing contacts and future employers is as important. This chapter discusses the value of follow-ups and offers practical methods for doing so with your network and potential employers.

What Makes Follow-Up Important?

Following-up in proactive manner can make a significant difference in your job hunt. It distinguishes you from the competition and demonstrates your unwavering excitement + sincere interest in the job. The need for follow-up is critical for a number of compelling reasons, including:

Underline Your Interest: A follow-up message or email serves to underline your genuine interest in the job/position, emphasising your dedication to pursuing the opportunity.

Maintain Your Presence in People's Minds: By following up, you can make sure that people in your network and employers will continue to think of you. It serves as a reminder of your candidature and profile.

Highlight Next Steps: Having a follow-up discussion will assist you understand the next steps in the hiring process and can also give you information about where you are among the other candidates.

Show Your Appreciation: A follow-up note gives you the chance to thank the individual you engaged with for their time and effort. It shows that you value their insightful opinions.

Don't hesitate/shy to Follow-Up: It's your moral responsibility to seek feedback & response upon your candidature. Don't think, will the recruiter get offended if you will keep doing a rigrous followup via emails or other means. Just think, there can be a scenario that they might not have seen your past email / msg followup. So, keep doing it until you get either a YES or a NO.

Additional Recommendations for Follow-Up Success:

Create a Plan: Establish the follow-up schedule and procedure, then start your rigrous followup until you get any update (either positive/negative). <u>Reach out them in every 2-3 days, use different timings to connect & also use different subject lines on existing mail chain to catch the attention of the recipient</u>. This demonstrates non-giving up attitude.

Professionalism and Courtesy: When following up, act in a courteous and dignified manner. In case they have forgotten who you are, introduce yourself briefly and use the recipient's first name while addressing them. Thank them for their time and consideration. Avoid sounding forceful or overly familiar with the employer as these things could turn them off.

Updates: Be careful to let the employer know if you've made any progress or reached any milestones since our last communication. For instance, emphasise your accomplishments if you have completed a project or a necessary certification. This demonstrates your initiative and unwavering dedication to your objectives.

Request Feedback: It might be beneficial to ask for feedback if the employer hasn't responded despite multiple follow-ups. Ask them politely if they have any suggestions for improvement or any reservations about your candidature. This shows that you are receptive to feedback and committed to developing your abilities.

4: PREPARE FOR INTERVIEWS:

"Preparation is the gateway to interview success."

Kudos for making it to the interview round! This is your chance to stand out and dazzle prospective employers. Employers use interviews to get to know you better and determine whether you're a good fit for the position. Although interviews can be anxiety-inducing, with the appropriate preparation and attitude, you can succeed and land your dream job. Here are a few pointers to help you get ready for interviews.

Conduct Company research:

Make sure you have done extensive research on the company before the interview. Learn about their main-stream business, mission, and core principles. You will be better able to understand the company's culture and how you may contribute to it with this insight.

Exercise with Regular Interview Questions:

Get ready for commonly asked interview questions, such as:

- Could you briefly describe who you are?
- Why are you motivated to work for this organisation?
- Why we should choose you over others?
- What is an example of a challenge you overcame?

To prevent memorising and achieve a confident delivery, practise your answers to these questions.

Make sure you are familiar with your resume.

Make sure you are completely comfortable with the information on your CV. Review your successes and experiences, and be prepared to talk about them. Be prepared for inquiries about your prior responsibilities and how they prepared you for the position you are applying for.

Check out the job description:

Examine the job description in detail and become familiar with its specifications. Learn the main duties and requirements for the position so that you can apply. This will provide you with the ability to respond to frequent interview questions about your qualifications and experience.

Create your inquiries:

When given the chance, prepare a list of questions to ask the interviewer. Ask about the corporate culture, the duties of the position, and you can even ask regarding the certifications/higher education preferences for the employees. This highlights your research and shows that you are interested in the job.

Show up early:

Prepare to get to the interview site at least 10 to 15 minutes early. You can use this time to unwind and collect your thoughts. Being on time indicates professionalism and minimises stress.

Acknowledge their involvement:

Send the interviewer an email or thank-you note after the interview. Thank them for their time and reiterate your interest in the position. This <u>distinguishes you as a strong applicant</u> over others by displaying your professionalism.

5: TAILOR YOUR RESUME & ATS:

"A tailored resume opens doors to opportunities."

Resumes are often the first point of contact between you and potential employers. Therefore, it's crucial to tailor your resume to match the specific requirements and preferences of each job application. This customization allows you to showcase your most relevant skills and experiences, increasing your chances of catching the employer's attention.

Start by thoroughly reviewing the job description and identifying keywords and skills the employer is seeking. Incorporate these keywords strategically throughout your resume, highlighting your proficiency in those areas. Use quantifiable achievements to demonstrate the impact you've made in previous roles.

Moreover, be mindful of **Applicant Tracking Systems** (ATS) used by many companies to screen resumes. ATS software scans your resumes with the job description for which you are applying. To ensure your resume passes this initial screening, format it in a clean and organized manner. Use standard fonts and avoid excessive formatting or complex layouts that may confuse the ATS.

Consider using bullet points to present your skills, experiences, and accomplishments. This format allows recruiters to quickly scan your resume and identify the relevant information. Finally, proofread your resume thoroughly to ensure it is error-free and presents you in the best possible light.

6: NETWORKING:

"Networking is the bridge that connects you to opportunities."

Building and nurturing a strong professional network can significantly expand your job search opportunities. Networking provides access to industry insights, job referrals, and hidden job market information.

Start by identifying relevant networking events, conferences, or online communities in your field. Attend industry-specific gatherings, join professional associations, and engage in online forums or social media groups. Actively participate in discussions, share valuable insights, and connect with like-minded professionals. Remember, networking is a two-way street, so be generous with your knowledge and support others in their professional endeavours.

Additionally, leverage your existing connections. Reach out to former colleagues, classmates, and mentors. Inform them about your job search goals and ask for advice or referrals. These personal connections can open doors to opportunities that may not be publicly advertised.

7: ASSESSING YOUR SKILLS:

"Know your skills, unlock your potential." [Usually we know everything about people around us, but we are not having the conscious awareness about our own patterns.] :P

Before embarking on a job search, take the time to assess your skills, strengths, and areas for development. This self-reflection will allow you to align your job search with your unique abilities and preferences.

Start by conducting a comprehensive skills inventory. Identify your hard skills, such as technical expertise, software proficiency, or industry-specific knowledge. Additionally, recognize your soft skills, including communication, leadership, problem-solving, and teamwork. This assessment will help you identify your unique selling points and articulate them effectively during interviews and in your resume.

Furthermore, consider seeking feedback from mentors, colleagues, or trusted individuals in your network. Their perspectives can provide valuable insights and help you uncover strengths and areas for improvement that you may have overlooked.

8: REFERRALS:

"Connections create opportunities."

Referrals can be a powerful tool in your job search toolkit. A referral from a trusted employee within an organization can significantly increase your chances of landing an interview and securing the job.

Reach out to your network and let them know about your job search goals. Inform them about the industries, companies, or positions you are targeting. If they have connections within those areas, kindly request introductions or referrals. Emphasize that you value their insights and would appreciate any assistance they can provide.

When approaching referrals, it's essential to be prepared and demonstrate your genuine interest in the company and role. Research the organization, prepare thoughtful questions, and be ready to articulate how your skills and experiences align with their needs.

"With the right strategies and a determined mindset, you have the power to unlock endless possibilities and shape your professional destiny."

KEY TAKEAWAYS:

- Ensure your professional profiles are optimized with relevant keywords and showcase your skills and accomplishments effectively. This will increase your visibility to potential employers.
- Take the initiative to follow up after submitting job applications or attending interviews.
- Customize your resume for each job application, make it ATS compliant. Highlighting relevant skills and experiences.
- Build and maintain professional relationships through networking. Attend industry events, join online communities, and engage with professionals to expand opportunities.
- Take time to assess your skills, strengths, and weaknesses. Identify areas for improvement and seek opportunities for growth and development.
- Leverage your network to seek referrals for job opportunities. Personal recommendations can carry significant weight and increase your chances of getting an interview.

Remember, the job search process can be competitive, but with the right mindset and actions, you can navigate it with confidence and achieve your career goals.

Chapter 3

MASTERING THE ART OF SALARY NEGOTIATION

The Blueprint for Successful Negotiations: Strategies and Techniques for closing the Deal

> *"By mastering the skill of negotiating, you can open the door to success and see your prospects grow."*

Unlimited opportunities exist in both the personal and professional domains. And negotiation skills are the key to unlocking them. Understanding this art is crucial for obtaining beneficial results in any situation, be it for a wage, a commercial agreement, or the resolution of a dispute. In this chapter, we'll examine the tactics and strategies that can help you develop as a negotiator, giving you the confidence and skills to handle challenging circumstances.

1: UNDERSTANDING YOUR WORTH

> *"Know your true value and unleash your negotiation prowess."*

Before entering into any discussions, it's critical to understand your value. This involves assessing your skills, knowledge, and credentials as well as the unique qualities that increase the value you can offer. Knowing your value assures you to effectively communicate your requests and approach discussions from a position of strength.

2: PREPARING FOR NEGOTIATIONS

> *"Preparation is the key to setup the deep foundation"*

Effective negotiation requires careful preparation to increase your chances of achieving favourable outcomes. Here are the key points covered in detail:

Gathering Relevant Information:

- **Identify the key issues:** Determine the main points of contention or areas that require negotiation.
- **Research and collect data:** Gather relevant information and facts that support your position and strengthen your arguments.
- **Understand the other party:** Gain insights into their interests, needs, and potential negotiation strategies.

Setting Clear Objectives:

- **Define your goals:** Determine what you want to accomplish and the specific outcomes you aim to achieve through the negotiation.
- **Prioritize your objectives:** Rank your objectives in order of importance, allowing you to focus on the most critical aspects.
- **Establish measurable criteria:** Define specific metrics or benchmarks that will indicate a successful negotiation.

Practising and Rehearsing:

- **Role-play negotiation scenarios:** Simulate the negotiation process to practice your arguments, responses, and counteroffers.
- **Seek feedback and refine your approach:** Engage in mock negotiations with colleagues or mentors to receive constructive feedback and improve your strategy.

By investing time in building a strong foundation allows you to approach discussions with confidence, adapt to unforeseen circumstances, and increase the likelihood of achieving your desired outcomes.

3: RARELY KNOWN CONCEPT UNDER SALARY NEGOTIATION

| **"Know Your Walk-Away Number"**

Establishing a defined bottom line, sometimes known as a "walk-away figure." This is a crucial aspect of negotiating, before engaging in any negotiation, decide on your walk-away number. It means that you will walk out, if the opponent will try to pull you below a certain amount/value that you decided as a bare minimum package in your mind. When you decide your Walk away number then you don't prefer going below this amount while sitting in the salary negotiation round with HR. This is the package below which you are reluctant to compromise.

But understand that, this is not your expected or desired salary, rather it's base level number. And you want anything above this threshold value (i.e Walk Away Number)

For Example: "Your current CTC is 10 Lakhs & your expectation to HR is 17 Lakhs. In this scenario, your walk away number can be 15 Lakhs, which means that if the HR will negotiate on 17L & tries to bring you down then, you wont go below 15 Lakhs and if HR will offer you something below your walk away number (i.e **15L** in this case), you will simply walk out & end the conversation."

If We are not moving in a planned way while negotiating our compensation, we will end up accepting the lower ctc offer letters.

"Differential Amount Negotiation"–Kickass Technique

This is something that will make you super effective while conversating with your leads/HR/Recruiters.It ideally means that you are having the discussion about the difference of what you are asking & what they are already intended to offer.

Let suppose: You are working on 5L ctc and you asked for 10L in the HR round of a new company. But the hr is offering you 9L instead of 10L. Now in this scenario the difference amount between your expectation and what they offer is (i.e 10L - 9L = **1L**).
So, you need to emphasize on the differential value i.e **1L** instead of talking about 10L.During your conversation, 10Lakh sounds bigger compared to just talking for an **extra 1Lakh**.

Hope it makes sense to you :) This technique is being used by almost every member of our community, along with hundreds of more such powerful ways And they are crushing it in their salary discussion rounds.

4: RESEARCH SALARY RANGES

"Knowledge is power - equip yourself with salary insights."

It's crucial to enter pay talks with correct and current compensation data in hand. When you undertake in-depth research to discover the salary ranges for employment in your industry and position, you obtain crucial insights. By being knowledgeable of market rates and industry norms, you can negotiate from a position of strength and demonstrate that you are aware of your value and the value you bring to the organisation. With this information, you may present stronger arguments and negotiate for a reasonable and market-based salary.

Platforms like:

- Glassdoor
- Payscale
- SalaryExpert
- These are popular sites that provide salary information based on user-reported data and market research. These platforms can give you an approximate idea of the salary ranges for a similar profile like you.

Additionally, leveraging your professional network, especially through platforms like LinkedIn, can be an efficient way to gather salary information. By connecting with individuals who work in the same company or industry, you can gain valuable insights about their salary ranges and compensation packages.

Use the information as a reference point but also keep in mind that negotiation should be based on a combination of market rates, your skills and experience, and the value you bring to the organization.

5: BUILDING EXPERIENTIAL STORIES

| *"Craft compelling narratives to convey your value."*

Storytelling can be a potent strategy for selling your value in negotiations. You can demonstrate your abilities, experiences, and accomplishments memorably and persuasively by sharing experiential stories. These anecdotes give specific examples of your past contributions, demonstrating your skills and authority. You may more easily explain and convince your opponents of the value you bring to the negotiation by creating appealing narratives that appeal to their emotions.

When crafting experiential stories to convey your value in interviews or negotiations, it's important to focus on adding value to the conversation. Instead of simply talking about your skills and capabilities, provide story-based examples that illustrate how you have utilized those skills to make a meaningful impact.

Experienced-based stories have the power to make a lasting impression on the interviewer or negotiation counterpart.

6: NEGOTIATING NON-SALARY BENEFITS:

"Perks Beyond Paycheck - Uncovering hidden opportunities."

Usually, compensation packages include more than just a wage. Be aware that non-salary benefits in compensation packages may be subject to negotiation. Determine and negotiate extra benefits like:

- Flexible work schedules
- Chances for career advancement & Certifications Reimbursement
- Health Insurance
- Joining Date extension with new employer
- Notice Period negotiation with the current employer
- Food Voucher

- Travel Allowance / Shift Allowance
- Joining Bonus (While entering the new company)

You can increase the value of your entire remuneration package and enhance your work-life balance by making use of these untapped negotiating possibilities.

7: DON'T GIVE A DEFINITE NUMBER - INSTEAD, USE A RANGE

| *"The power of flexibility in negotiation."*

While discussing salary in the recruiter, flexibility is a significant advantage. Offering a range rather than a fixed amount turns out to be super efficient. By using a range, you give yourself more leverage during the negotiating process for debate.

Finding novel solutions and achieving win-win outcomes are two more advantages of providing a range. Allowing for discussion within a range creates the possibility of finding original solutions that satisfy the demands and interests of both parties. This strategy can result in the discovery of perfect answers that could have gone unnoticed if only a precise number was given.

To provide an example, imagine that you are expected to earn 12 Lakhs CTC. You can give a range, such as 11 LPA to 13 LPA, rather than declaring a fixed amount. This range offers additional room for negotiating, allowing the employer to take into account different choices within the predetermined range. Now, you have an option of even pushing them towards 13 Lakhs as well, if they sound confident with your so far performances. Additionally, it leaves an opportunity for possible alterations in light of many other issues raised during the negotiation process.

Engaging Scenario-Based Questions:

Let's examine some typical situations where negotiation abilities are essential and look at the remedies that can assist you handle them successfully. You may negotiate these circumstances with confidence and raise your chances of getting the results you want by being aware of the methods and approaches used.

A: You have been offered a job with a lower salary than expected. How can you negotiate for a higher compensation package?
Solution: Create a compelling argument by highlighting your abilities, credentials, and the value you can offer to the company. Support your proposal with market research and instances of your successes. Examining non-salary benefits during negotiations can greatly improve your overall compensation package in addition to resolving the pay gap. These intangible perks can increase job satisfaction and show that you have a comprehensive approach to pay.

Maintain a cooperative and respectful demeanour during the negotiation process, concentrating on achieving an agreement that benefits everyone.

B: Imagine you are facing objections during a negotiation. How would you address those concerns, reframe perspectives, and establish a common ground to navigate the objections skillfully?
During negotiations, it's crucial to handle objections skillfully. First, actively listen without interruption to the other party's objections.

Show respect and create an open communication environment. Next, validate their concerns and demonstrate empathy.

Reframe perspectives by offering alternative viewpoints, supported by facts and examples. Provide fresh insights/references to encourage considering new solutions. Establish common ground by identifying shared interests and goals.

Avoid being defensiveness and aim for win-win outcomes. By employing active listening, empathy, and a problem-solving mindset, you can effectively navigate objections and increase the likelihood of achieving desired outcomes.

> *"Mastering the art of negotiation empowers you to shape your destiny, forge meaningful connections, and seize the outcomes you truly desire."*

KEY TAKEAWAYS:

- Understanding your worth is essential for effective negotiation.
- Thorough preparation and research lay the foundation for successful negotiations.
- Crafting compelling narratives and using effective communication techniques can enhance your negotiation skills.
- Responding to counteroffers, negotiating non-salary benefits, and overcoming objections are key strategies for achieving favourable outcomes.
- Setting boundaries with a walk-away number and using a range instead of a definite number can provide flexibility in negotiations.
- Shifting perspectives and creating reverse realizations can influence positive outcomes.

Remember, Negotiation is a skill that can be honed with practice and experience. By mastering the art of negotiation, you can open a new world of possibilities and achieve desired outcomes in various aspects of your life.

Chapter 4

10 THINGS NOT TO DO IN A JOB SEARCH PROCESS

> *"Your Job Search Process is a journey; avoid the wrong turns to reach your dream destination."*

Starting a job hunt can be a difficult task full of obstacles and unknowns. It's a path that calls for cautious navigation, calculated choices, and the capacity to communicate your abilities and qualities. To increase your chances of success, it's critical to concentrate on what you should do, but it's also critical to be aware of **what not to do**. We will examine critical mistakes in this chapter that will make your journey fail-proof.

The job search process is a dynamic and constantly changing environment, impacted by elements including technological breakthroughs, shifting industry trends, and changing employer expectations. You can overcome these obstacles and improve your chances of landing your dream job by being proactive and knowledgeable.

Let's examine the dos and don'ts of the job search process so that we can better equip ourselves to make wise choices, avoid frequent pitfalls, and set out on a path to a career that will be both meaningful and rewarding.

1: THE HARSH REALITY OF COVER LETTERS:

> *"The Significance of cover letter has evolved widely, it has a different meaning now compared to a decade before"*

Several factors contribute to the changing emphasis placed on cover letters by hiring managers and recruiters. **Time constraints** play a vital role as these professionals have limited time to review applications, often <u>giving priority to only resume</u> as their primary reference point.

Another factor is most recruiters do not consider cover letters as a primary factor in the selection process. Instead, they focus more on evaluating a candidate's persona, which showcases their relevant experience, skills, qualifications, certifications, confidence etc.

But yes, applying with cover letter does **make a lot of sense when applying for positions outside of India**. Profiles with cover letters tend to hold more weight. However, in the Indian job market, this doesn't hold true.

Still if you choose to include a cover letter in your application, it is crucial to make it **personalized** and impactful. *"A customized cover letter speaks volumes; a generic one gets lost in the shuffle."*

In just a few lines, convey your unique value proposition and demonstrate a genuine understanding of the company's needs. Craft a compelling opening that grabs the reader's attention and highlights your relevant qualifications.

2: CRAFTING A PROFESSIONAL RESUME: AVOIDING COMMON PITFALLS

"An attention grabbing resume is all you need, to authoritate your journey and experiences."

When it comes to crafting a resume, there are certain things you should avoid to ensure a professional and compelling presentation. Here are some key areas to pay attention to:

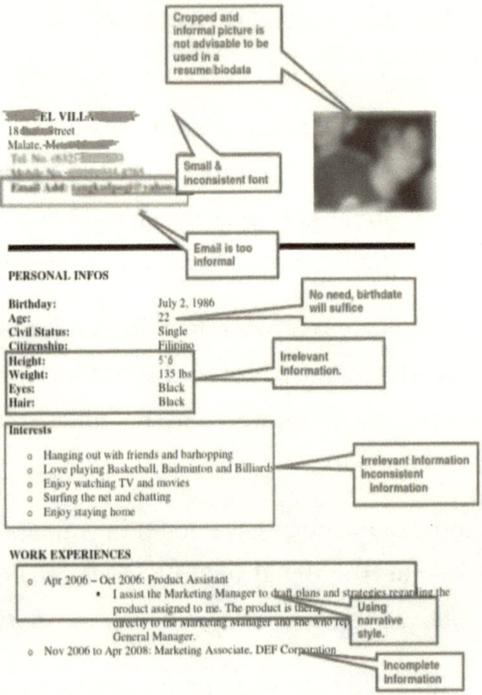

Unprofessional Email IDs: Avoid using personal or unprofessional email IDs that might leave a negative impression on potential employers. Opt for a straightforward email address that includes your name.

Unprofessional Photograph: Including a photograph in your resume can be optional. However, if you choose to include one, ensure that it is a professional-looking photo. **Avoid** using pictures with low lighting, party pictures, or any images that may give off an unprofessional impression. Dress professionally and maintain a neutral facial expression.

Content in Tabular Format: Traditional tabular formats in your profile are no longer favoured in the current job market.

Instead, focus on creating a visually appealing and easy-to-read resume by using bullet points and concise paragraphs. Highlight your practical exposures and personal growth throughout your professional journey.

Avoid Overemphasizing Career Gaps: If you have gaps in your employment history, it's important talk about it, when asked but no need to overemphasize them on your resume.

Too Much Text and Lack of Spacing: A cluttered resume with excessive text can be overwhelming and difficult to read. Ensure appropriate spacing and use bullet points or short paragraphs to make the content easily scannable. This helps maintain the reader's interest and allows them to quickly grasp the key information.

3: NEGLECTING NETWORKING: BUILDING RELATIONSHIPS FOR SUCCESS

> *"Networking is not just a buzzword; it's a powerful tool for unlocking hidden opportunities."*

Neglecting the value of networking is one of the blunders job searchers make most frequently. Since many jobs are filled through recommendations and relationships, networking is a very useful skill. By extending your professional network, you have access to untapped job prospects and industry insider knowledge.

Join professional meetups, attend industry events, participate in other networking activities. Ask for informational interviews with experts in the subject you want to work in, so you may benefit from their knowledge and recommendations.

Keep in mind that networking is a two-way process, so be prepared to extend the same courtesy to others. Making genuine connections can result in recommendations, job referrals, and a more robust professional network.

4: AVOIDING AN EMPTY PROFILE: MAXIMIZING YOUR LINKEDIN POTENTIAL

> *"Your LinkedIn profile is your digital representative in the professional world. Don't let major blunders hinder your chances of making a lasting impression"*

Your LinkedIn page is more than just an online CV; it's a doorway to success, connections, and career chances. However, some errors can make it more difficult for you to stand out and attract the interest of recruiters, employers, and possible contacts.

The biggest mistakes to avoid on your LinkedIn profile will be covered in this article, enabling you to build a flawless online identity that best represents your professionalism, knowledge, and objectives. You may make the most of LinkedIn and open up a world of job opportunities by avoiding these mistakes.

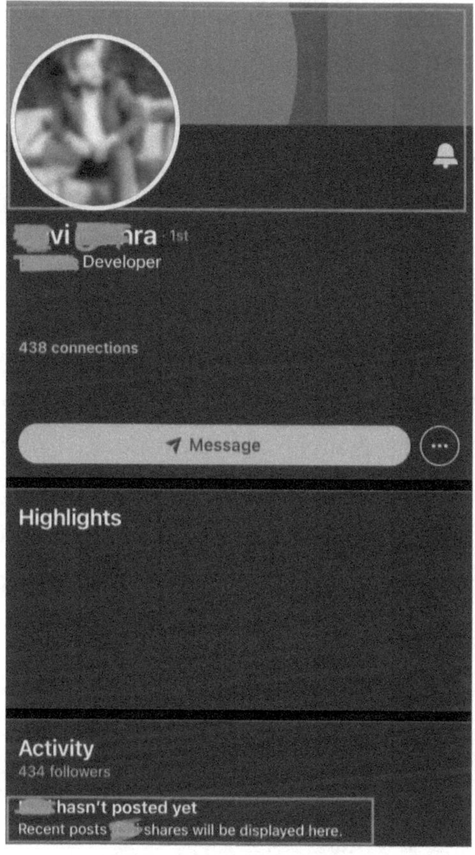

Missing COVER IMAGE on your Profile: The cover image on your LinkedIn profile is a valuable visual element that should not be overlooked. It serves as the first impression for anyone visiting your profile and can significantly impact how your candidature is perceived. By having a well-chosen cover image, you can add clarity to your profile and make it appear more serious and qualifying. Consider using a professional image that aligns with your industry or personal brand to create a visually appealing and engaging first impression.

No Detailed "ABOUT" Section: The "About" section on your LinkedIn profile provides an opportunity to give visitors a deeper understanding of your professional background, skills, and career goals. Neglecting to provide a detailed summary can be a major blunder. This section allows you to showcase your expertise, highlight key achievements, and communicate your unique value proposition.

Haven't posted/shared anything on your LinkedIn profile: LinkedIn is not just a static resume repository; it's also a platform for professional engagement and networking. Failing to post or share anything on your LinkedIn profile can convey a msg of nonactive profile. Sharing valuable content regularly can also help attract the attention of recruiters and potential employers, as well as establish your credibility as a thought leader in your industry.

"Avoiding these major blunders on your LinkedIn profile is crucial for presenting a strong and professional online presence."

5: LACK OF STRATEGIC JOB SEARCHING: MOVING BEYOND QUANTITY

"In the vast sea of job opportunities, result lies not in the number of applications you send, but in the strategic choices you make."

When embarking on a job search, it may be tempting to cast a wide net and apply to every available position that catches your eye. However, adopting a "spray and pray" approach can often be counterproductive and lead to a waste of time and energy.

Instead, it's crucial to approach your job search with a strategic mindset and be selective in the positions you choose to apply for.

Define Your Career Goals: Before diving into the job market, take the time to clarify your career goals and aspirations. What type of role are you seeking? What industries or companies align with your interests and values? By having a clear understanding of your career objectives, you can narrow down your focus and target specific opportunities that are in line with your long-term goals.

Quality Over Quantity: Applying to every available position can dilute your efforts and hinder your chances of success. Instead, prioritize quality over quantity. Focus on positions that truly align with your skills, experience, and career goals. By putting conscious effort into a smaller number of applications, you can increase your chances of standing out and being considered a strong candidate.

Research and Target Companies: Take the time to research and identify companies that align with your career aspirations. Look for organizations that share your values, have a positive work culture, and offer opportunities for growth and development.

Seek Quality Feedback: Receiving feedback throughout your job search can be invaluable. If you consistently face rejections or fail to secure interviews, it may be an indication that you need to refine your approach. Seek feedback from mentors, career advisors, or industry professionals who can provide insights and suggestions for improvement. Use this feedback to fine-tune your job search strategy.

Remember, the job search process is not about applying to every available position but rather about strategically identifying and pursuing opportunities that align with your career goals.

6: IGNORING ONLINE PRESENCE: THE POWER AND PERILS OF SOCIAL MEDIA

"Your online presence can make or break your job search; use it wisely."

In the modern digital era, your online presence is crucial to the success of your job search. Unfortunately, a lot of job searchers disregard their online identity by publishing improper material that could damage their reputation in the industry. Like useless memes, political content etc.

Start by doing a complete assessment of your social media profiles to prevent these traps. Check your privacy settings to make sure that only the intended audiences may see your personal information. Remove anything that could be damaging or unprofessional, such as insulting words, improper images, or critical remarks about prior employers.

Utilise social media to help with your job search at the same time. Make a strong LinkedIn profile that highlights your abilities, background, and achievements. To show your knowledge, interact with others in your profession, share articles or insights that are relevant to your sector.

Keep in mind that social media profiles are frequently accessed by companies to learn more about candidates. To improve your chances of generating a good impression, conduct yourself professionally and positively.

7: FAILING TO EXPRESS GRATITUDE: THANK-YOU EMAIL

"A simple thank-you note can leave a lasting impression, turning an interview into a memorable connection and setting yourself apart in the competitive job market."

In today's competitive job market, standing out from the crowd requires more than just acing an interview. It's the small gestures, like sending a well-crafted thank-you note or email, that can leave a lasting impression on potential employers. Don't underestimate the power of expressing your gratitude and professionalism after each interview.

Timing is Key: Don't let time slip away after the interview. Aim to send your thank-you note or email within 24-48 hours to ensure it arrives while your conversation is still fresh in the interviewer's mind. Promptness demonstrates your keen interest and attention to detail.

Personalization Matters: Avoid generic templates and make your message stand out by personalizing it. Refer to specific details discussed during the interview or any unique aspects that resonated with you. This personal touch showcases your active listening skills and reinforces your genuine interest in the position.

Express Sincere Gratitude: Begin your thank-you note by expressing your heartfelt appreciation for the opportunity to interview. Let the interviewer(s) know that you value their time and consideration. Gratitude sets a positive tone and demonstrates your professionalism and courtesy.

Reiterate Your Interest: Take the opportunity to reaffirm your enthusiasm for the role and the organization. Emphasize why you believe you are the right fit for the position, highlighting your relevant skills and experiences. Show how your contributions can positively impact the company's success.

Share Contact Information: To make it easy for the interviewers to reach out to you, must include your contact information at the end of your note.

"Don't forget to send this note after your next interview conversation".

8: NEGLECTING PROFESSIONAL DEVELOPMENT: LIFELONG LEARNING FOR SUCCESS

"Invest in yourself; the dividends will pay off in your job search and beyond."

Some job seekers disregard the value of continuing professional development in favour of concentrating only on completing applications and attending interviews. This strategy may make it more difficult for you to stand out from the crowd of applicants who make a conscious effort to advance their education and training.

Continuous professional development keeps you informed of market trends and best practices while also demonstrating your dedication to improvement. Utilise conferences, workshops, webinars, and online courses that are relevant to your professional objectives. Look for certifications or other credentials that will strengthen your resume and help you stand out from the crowd.

In interviews, while talking about professional development, focus on particular occasions where you actively sought out learning opportunities. Showcase how your skill set has grown as a result of these events to make yourself a stronger candidate for the job.

You may impress potential employers with your commitment to developing and remaining competitive by investing in your professional development.

9: FAILING IN RIGOROUS FOLLOW-UP:

"Success is often achieved by those who are willing to put in the extra effort and follow up relentlessly."

The job search process doesn't end with the interview in the cutthroat world of the job market. It's just the beginning of a crucial phase: the follow-up. Don't make the mistake of neglecting this important step in the hiring process. By being proactive, professional, and persistent in your follow-up efforts, you can significantly enhance your chances of standing out and securing the job.

Demonstrate Continued Interest: Following up with interviewers is a powerful way to demonstrate your continued interest in the position. Express your gratitude for the opportunity to interview and reiterate your enthusiasm for the role and the company. Use this opportunity to address any outstanding questions or provide additional information that might reinforce your candidacy.

Doing rigorous followup <u>does not mean that you are being desperate for the position</u> rather when you are showcasing your continuous interest in a positive way, you are always preferred over other applicants.

Be Patient, But Not Passive: Patience is essential when waiting for a response from interviewers. Understand that hiring decisions often take time due to various factors within the company. Follow up at appropriate intervals converts really well.

By implementing a rigorous follow-up strategy, you showcase your professionalism, enthusiasm, and commitment. You demonstrate your proactive nature and strong determination & perseverance.

10: NEGLECTING SELF-CARE: MANAGING STRESS AND AVOIDING BURNOUT +

"Take care of yourself, and your job search will follow suit."

Many people overlook their well-being during a job search since it can be emotionally draining and uncertain. Self-care should be prioritised because neglecting it can result in increased stress, fatigue, and a decreased capacity to project confidence in interviews.

Self-care should be a top concern when you are looking for a job. By establishing boundaries and allotting time for rest, hobbies, exercise, and quality time with loved ones, you may achieve a healthy work-life balance. Utilise ways for reducing stress, such as deep breathing exercises, meditation, or happy pursuits.

Ask for assistance from your loved ones, your friends, or career mentors as well. Talk to those who can guide and inspire you about your worries, anxieties, and accomplishments. Sharing your experiences with others can help you relax.

It's important to keep in mind that taking care of your physical, mental, and emotional needs is not selfish but rather essential to your resilience and ability to remain upbeat throughout the job search process.

"Stay focused, stay determined, and remember: you're just one step away from your breakthrough.

KEY TAKEAWAYS:

- Tailor each cover letter to the specific job and company, showcasing your unique skills and qualifications.
- Build relationships, attend industry events, and seek out opportunities for referrals and connections.
- Audit your social media profiles, remove unprofessional content, and leverage platforms like LinkedIn to showcase your expertise.
- Continually improve your skills and knowledge through courses, certifications, and workshops to stand out among other candidates.
- Leave your current job on good terms, maintain positive relationships, and leverage connections for future opportunities.
- Manage stress, maintain work-life balance, and seek support to stay resilient and motivated during your job search.

By keeping these key takeaways in mind, you can navigate the job search process effectively, increase your chances of success, and find the right career opportunity that aligns with your aspirations.

Chapter 5

INSANE PROFILE OPTIMISATION, RECRUITERS CAN'T AVOID

Here, We will talk about how to maximise Your opportunities on Naukri and LinkedIn in a unique way.

1: ENHANCING YOUR PROFESSIONAL PROFILE WITH VIDEO RESUMES:

"This will Boost Your Job Search and Ignite Your Career Journey."

Video resumes are a game-changer in a competitive job market, increasing interview call-backs by an astonishing fivefold. Surprisingly, over 98 per cent of job searchers are losing out on this ground-breaking strategy. Thankfully, popular sites like LinkedIn and Naukri have embraced this functionality, giving you a chance to stand out among the top 2%.

Remember: Naukri's recruiters highly prefer those profiles that contain videos for their resumes.

Create a concise video resume that lasts between 60 and 90 seconds if you want to create the biggest impression. In this limited amount of time, you can give a compelling review of your background, notable accomplishments, and areas of strength. Numerous members of our community have experienced spectacular increases in their interview calls & High CTC 0ffers ranging from 100% to an astounding 500% Hike by utilising the power of video resumes.

Don't let this powerful tool slip through your fingers.

2: DON'T UNDERESTIMATE YOUR PROFILE HEADLINE/SUMMARY! ITS NOT JUST A SIMPLE TEXT

(Mohini is one of our mentees)

Your LinkedIn and Naukri headline/summary is more than a simple text on a profile; it serves as your online introduction and pitch. It can grab reader's interest, give a brief overview of who you are, and make your value clear to employers or clients. (*Like - You can clearly get to know about mohini by just looking at her profile snapshot*)

Reader should get a helicopter view of your core strengths & authority of your candidature by reading your headline/summary.

Regarding the significance of editing and polishing, paying close attention to detail is essential to produce a polished, error-free content. Add your unique personality to your summary to make it stand out from the crowd.

3: UNDERSTANDING THE POWER OF STORYTELLING:

"Your summary is your story—craft it with deep exposure & captivate your audience."

People are enthralled by stories. Storytelling has always been a potent technique for eliciting feelings, creating connections, and making knowledge remember. You can use storytelling to captivate your audience and make a positive impression on LinkedIn and Naukri.

Creating Emotions: Stories have a special power to arouse feelings and foster empathy. You can establish a stronger connection with your readers by incorporating storytelling aspects by including personal struggles, victories or past project examples.

Establishing Contacts: By highlighting shared experiences, ideals, and aspirations, stories help people feel more connected. Create a summary that reflects the experiences and goals of your target audience and incorporate relatable stories to encourage others to interact with your profile.

Relatability: Stories are relatable because they feature characters, circumstances, or difficulties that people can identify with. You give others the chance to relate to you personally by sharing your path, experiences, and personal development. This relatability promotes authenticity and trust, which push people to get in touch with you.

Use storytelling to elicit feelings, forge relationships, and leave a lasting impression in your profile. You may attract the enormous possibilities and build lasting contacts on LinkedIn and Naukri by emphasising your key insights.

4: SHOWCASING IMPACTFUL ACHIEVEMENTS:

> *"Don't just list your accomplishments—showcase the impact you've made."*

Simply listing your accomplishments won't cut it when it comes to showing them in the overview. You must emphasise the contribution you made in your past roles. Focus on measuring your accomplishments and displaying quantifiable results rather than merely listing your accomplishments.

Did you contribute to a specific % rise in sales/productivity/ efficiency of your past project/company? Did you succeed in streamlining procedures and saving the business time or money?

By presenting verifiable proof of your efforts, you build credibility and show what a new project can gain from you.

It's also important to highlight how your achievements have helped your group or organisation succeed. Include collaborations, leadership responsibilities, or projects where you had a major impact. Showcase how your actions have improved results, fueled growth, or overcome obstacles.

You position yourself as a valuable asset to potential employers or clients by demonstrating that you are not simply an individual achiever but also someone who can have a significant impact within a bigger framework.

5: INCORPORATING KEYWORDS AND SKILLS:

"Strategically include relevant keywords to enhance your visibility and searchability."

It's crucial to strategically incorporate effective keywords and abilities into your summary to improve your exposure and searchability on websites like LinkedIn and Naukri. Find the keywords that resonate with your target audience, industry-specific terminologies.

However, when adding keywords, it's crucial to maintain a balance. It's important to optimise your summary for search engine algorithms, but it's also important to keep your summary readable and in a professional tone. Avoid overloading your summary with keywords, which will make it seem forced and artificial. You may do this to make your profile more visible in searches while maintaining reader engagement and connection.

You can position yourself as a capable professional and improve your chances of getting the correct prospects by emphasising significant accomplishments and strategically incorporating pertinent keywords and abilities. Keep in mind that the objective is to highlight the value you bring to the table and make it simple for prospective employers or clients to locate and contact you.

6: ENGAGING THE READER'S EMOTIONS

> *"Make an emotional connection by sharing your values, passions, and aspirations."*

It's crucial to go beyond simply listing your qualifications and professional accomplishments to make a lasting impression with your description. A more genuine and profound connection can be made by appealing to the reader's emotions. To humanise your profile and demonstrate the motivations behind your job, share your values, hobbies, and objectives.

Describe your motivation for doing what you do and how it ties in with your basic values. To show your sincere excitement, share personal anecdotes or events that have influenced your path. You can push people and draw organisations / professionals who share your values and goals by showcasing the deeper purpose underlying your work.

Furthermore, declaring your ambitions might demonstrate your dedication to lifelong learning and development. Describe the difference you hope to make in your industry or the constructive change you wish to see in society. By sharing your goals with others, you create a sense of shared purpose.

You make a more lasting and meaningful impression when you emotionally engage your audience. A profile that stirs up feelings and connects with the reader's values and interests is more likely to be remembered and generate interest.

7: PROOFREADING AND POLISHING

"Attention to detail is crucial—ensure your content is error-free and presents you in the best light."

Before posting your profile content, it's important to pay close attention to the last-minute details, make sure it's error-free, and make sure it accurately represents you. To avoid having your professionalism and trustworthiness damaged by typos, grammatical mistakes, or poor wording, proofreading is crucial.

Spend some time carefully reading the overview and reviewing it for spelling and grammar errors. Think about employing tools for proofreading or having a reliable friend or coworker look through your content as well. They can provide new perspectives and provide insightful criticism or suggestions for advancement.

Keep in mind that your profile frequently serves as your initial impression to prospective employers or clients. Make sure it conveys your devotion to excellence and attention to detail because it sets the tone for the remainder of your profile. A flawless and well-written summary demonstrate professionalism and inspires faith in your capacity.

8: PERSONALIZING YOUR SUMMARY:

Tagline: "Make your summary uniquely yours by injecting your personality and authentic voice."

Your summary is a chance for you to highlight your personality and leave an enduring impression. Maintaining a professional tone is crucial, but don't be afraid to add your real voice/flavour and allow your personality to come through. Use words and phrases that are authentic to you and your style of communication.

Avoid utilising cliches and generic buzzwords that could make your overview sound generic or identical to many others. Instead, be authentic to your professional brand when expressing yourself. Let your writing reflect your energy, passion, and distinct viewpoint. This personal touch makes your summary stand out from the competition and forges a stronger, more sincere bond with your readers.

9: INCORPORATING MULTIMEDIA AND VISUALS:

"Enhance your profile with multimedia to make it visually appealing."

In addition to well-crafted text, consider incorporating multimedia and visuals to make your summary visually appealing. Your summary's aesthetic appeal and the overall effect can be greatly improved by adding multimedia and pictures.

Visual Appeal: You can improve the visual appeal and readability of your summary by including few images. The inclusion of certification thumbnails or logos of the companies/clients that you had worked for, can draw viewer's attention right away and set your profile apart from the competition.

Links to Related Projects: You can offer concrete proof of your work by including links to related projects, articles, or presentations. This not only shows readers your abilities and knowledge but also encourages them to learn more about you and your achievements.

Putting Your Abilities and Achievements on Display: Images are best to showcase your abilities and accomplishments on display. You can add certain initiatives, emphasise your skills, or show the influence you've had. These visual representations assist make your accomplishments come to life and leave a more a deeper impression.

You may give your viewers an appealing and engaging experience by including multimedia and pictures in your summary. This catches attention and gives a more dynamic portrayal of your abilities and accomplishments.

"Craft your profile content that captivates, connects, and compels—your gateway to success on LinkedIn and Naukri."

KEY TAKEAWAYS:

- Create a captivating narration in your synopsis that appeals to your intended audience.
- Display not only your successes but also the contribution you made in earlier positions or projects. Put a number on your accomplishments and emphasise measurable outcomes.
- Share your passions, ideals, and objectives to establish an emotional connection. Make your profile more personable to make a good impression.
- Make your summary unique by adding your individuality and true voice, which should reflect who you are as a professional.
- To keep your summary current and pertinent, seek input from reliable sources and make revisions as needed.
- Add multimedia and pictures to your summary to make it more eye-catching and to highlight your efforts.

Applying these essential ideas can help you improve your summary so that it tells a captivating and succinct tale, attracting more chances and raising your profile on LinkedIn and Naukri.

Chapter 6

CAREER BRANDING

Crafting Your Professional Identity for Success

> *"Your brand serves as a professional compass that directs you towards success and helps you stand out from the competition."*

In today's fast-paced and hyper-competitive job market, where opportunities are often limited and the pool of qualified candidates is vast, understanding the power of career branding has become essential to professional success. To make a lasting impression and stand out in the middle of intense competition, professionals today need to go beyond the conventional measures.

This chapter will go in-depth on how to create and manage a powerful personal brand that accurately represents your professional identity. As we accompany you on a transformative journey of self-discovery, we will help you gain a complete understanding of your brand and how it relates to your professional goals. You can create a captivating presence that reflects your genuine-self and connects with your target audience by investigating your passions, values, and strengths.

1: BUILDING YOUR ONLINE PRESENCE

> *"Your online presence is your digital storefront – make it attractive, authentic, and engaging."*

Employers and recruiters increasingly turn to the Internet to research and evaluate potential candidates before making hiring decisions. Building an impressive online presence not only increases your visibility but also allows you to showcase your expertise, professionalism, and unique value proposition.

Professional Branding: Establishing a Cohesive Identity

Professional branding refers to the intentional development and promotion of a consistent and cohesive identity for individuals in the corporate world. It involves strategically defining and showcasing one's skills, credentials, and values to prospective employers. By effectively crafting and communicating a professional brand, individuals can establish a strong personal brand that sets them apart from others and enhances their career prospects.

This entails several processes, including recognising individual talents, outlining professional objectives, matching them to desired roles, and creating a compelling personal brand statement that grabs recruiters' attention.

2: OPTIMIZING LINKEDIN: THE PROFESSIONAL'S PLATFORM

Utilising LinkedIn strategically to improve professional visibility, networking opportunities, and career possibilities is part of optimising the platform for corporate professionals. This involves maximising the impact of your LinkedIn profile by highlighting your talents, accomplishments, and aspirations in important sections like the headline, name title, summary, and experience.

Corporate professionals can effectively position themselves as industry experts, grow their professional networks, and improve their chances of landing new opportunities and moving forward in their professions by utilising LinkedIn's features and resources.

Showcasing Professional Achievements: Portfolios and Case Studies

By showcasing their professional accomplishments through case studies and portfolios, individuals may show off their knowledge, abilities, and successful projects. Portfolios are carefully organised sets of work samples that offer verifiable proof of skills and achievements. Professionals can attract new prospects in their fields by effectively communicating their worth, experience, and capacity to achieve exceptional results through the presentation of portfolios and case studies.

3: BUILDING YOUR REPUTATION AND CREDIBILITY

> *"Your reputation precedes you — cultivate it with integrity, professionalism, and excellence."*

Your professional reputation and believability are crucial in determining the course of your career. Consistency, integrity, and a dedication to producing outstanding results are necessary for developing a solid reputation. How to build a solid professional reputation, get the respect and trust of your coworkers and peers in the business, and establish your credibility as a trustworthy and capable professional. You can create strong networks, gain access to new opportunities, and improve your career in a meaningful and long-lasting way by taking care of your reputation and credibility.

Professional Networking:

To increase the size of your professional network, cultivate genuine relationships both online and offline. Attend industry conferences, seminars, and events to network with like-minded people and possible partners. To increase your network and create worthwhile connections, join professional communities of like-minded people that will help advance your career.

Testimonials and Recommendations:

Look for endorsements and testimonials from clients, coworkers, and mentors who have personally witnessed the value of your work. These recommendations boost your personal brand's reputation and act as strong social proof. To inspire trust and confidence in potential employers or clients, make them visible on your online platforms, such as your website or LinkedIn page.

Continuous Learning:

Adopt a philosophy of lifelong learning and invest in your professional growth. Join workshops, seminars, or conferences, pursue pertinent certifications, and enrol in courses to broaden your knowledge base and learn new abilities. To remain competitive in your profession, keep up with market trends, technology developments, and best practices. You show your dedication to excellence, adaptability, and staying on top of trends by constantly learning and developing, which makes you a sought-after professional in the eyes of both employers and clients.

4: SOFT SKILLS

"Soft Skills, which go beyond technical proficiency, are the fundamentals of a successful career,"

Strong soft skills are vital for career success in today's networked and people-focused organisations. Numerous qualities, including communication, teamwork, adaptability, and emotional intelligence, are included in the category of soft skills. We will go into the importance of acquiring and polishing these vital skills in this part.

By developing your soft skills, you will not only be more productive when working with others but also set yourself out as a well-rounded professional who can handle difficult situations and promote change.

Communication Skills:

Master the art of effective communication, both verbal and written. Develop active listening skills, practice clarity and conciseness, and adapt your communication style to different audiences.

Emotional Intelligence:

Cultivate self-awareness, empathy, and the ability to manage emotions. Understand and navigate interpersonal dynamics, resolve conflicts, and build strong relationships with colleagues and clients.

Leadership and Collaboration:

Demonstrate leadership qualities, foster teamwork, and collaborate effectively with others. Develop skills in decision-making, problem-solving, and conflict resolution to thrive in diverse professional environments.

Gestures & Actions:

How do you behave, act & respond among people matters a lot. Your natural instinct reflects how do you think & react to the normal day to day situations. And also your facial expressions has a huge role to depict your personality.

5: PRESENTATION SKILLS

"Captivate, Connect, and Conquer the Room with Masterful Presentations!"

The ability to communicate ideas, sway opinions, and make a lasting impression on your audience is made possible by effective presentation abilities, which are invaluable in a variety of professional contexts. This part will look at how to deliver engaging presentations that captivate your audience.

Structuring Your Presentation:

Creating an impactful presentation involves structuring it logically, engaging the audience, and utilizing nonverbal communication effectively. Consider these key areas:

Structure: Craft an attention-grabbing introduction and organize your content with clear headings and subheadings. This helps guide the audience and ensures a coherent flow.

Engagement: Move beyond facts and figures by incorporating interactive elements like visual aids, storytelling, and real-life examples. Encourage participation and make the presentation memorable.

Nonverbal Communication: Pay attention to body language, gestures, and facial expressions. Maintain an open posture, use purposeful gestures, and convey appropriate emotions to establish rapport and connect with the audience.

By focusing on effective structure, engaging elements, and impactful nonverbal communication, you'll deliver a presentation that resonates with your audience and effectively conveys your message.

6: CONTENT AUTHORITY

"Establish yourself as a trusted expert in your field and build your authority through valuable content posting."

Establishing content authority is essential for professionals looking to be recognised as reliable sources of knowledge and expertise in today's information-driven environment. Your position as an industry leader is strengthened by your content authority, which attracts opportunities and shapes opinions. The creation of outstanding content, the wise use of digital channels, and engagement with your target audience are all methods we'll examine to help you build and strengthen your content authority.

Research and Expertise:

By devoting time to rigorous study and becoming current with industry trends, you can enhance your brand. You can establish yourself as an authority in your subject by expanding your knowledge. To build credibility and draw a devoted following, share well-researched insights and professional viewpoints through blog entries, articles, or social media content. You will develop a reputation as a reliable information source by showcasing your expertise, which will open doors to intriguing opportunities and collaborations.

Thought Leadership:

Your years of experience is not the only factor that proves you a Thought Leader in a respective field, rather You can position yourself as a respected authority in your field by actively participating in professional conversation & sharing relevant content to people.

Look for chances to share your knowledge, whether it be through writing pieces for trade journals, giving presentations at conferences, or taking part in panel discussions. You position yourself as a go-to resource in your industry by sharing your viewpoints and experiences. Your brand as a thought leader will be established if you consistently produce high-quality material, such as thought-provoking blog articles or captivating films, and participate in important discussions online and offline.

7: BUILDING A PROFESSIONAL IMAGE

"Elevate your professional presence and make a lasting impression with a strong and polished image."

Your brand is visually represented by your professional image, which makes an impression on everyone you come into contact with. This section looks at practical methods for creating and maintaining a professional image that supports your brand and broadens your employment options.

Personal Appearance:

Pay close attention to how you look generally, including how you are dressed and how you are groomed. When dressing for various situations, make sure to represent your business and the industry you work in with your sense of style. You may command respect and exude confidence in any professional setting by presenting a polished and professional image.

Online Etiquette:

Maintaining a professional demeanour at all times when interacting online is proper internet etiquette. Through appropriate use of social media, respectful email correspondence, and deliberate online networking, keep up a consistent and pleasant online image. Keep in mind that how others view you depends significantly on your internet presence, which is an extension of your professional image.

Networking and Relationship Building:

Develop trusting, real relationships in your professional life. To grow your network, take part in deliberate networking activities like going to industry events or joining organisations for professionals. Develop these connections by being supportive, sharing insightful information, and giving back to the industry. Building a solid reputation among your peers and business leaders will improve your professional image and lead to more chances.

8: CREATING AN ACTION PLAN

"Chanelize your career branding success with a personalized action plan."

Now that you have explored various aspects of career branding, it's time to create an action plan to implement what you have learned. In this section, we will guide you through the process of creating a personalized action plan to take your career branding efforts to the next level.

Setting Goals:

Establish measurable objectives for your professional branding journey. Determine the milestones you want to reach and create time frames that are reasonable for doing so. By establishing specific goals, you give your professional branding efforts a clear direction and a road map to success.

Prioritizing Actions:

Your objectives should be broken down into manageable, significant actions. Set these steps in order of importance and make sure they are in line with your overall career goals. You may maximise your efforts and assure progress towards your targeted goals by concentrating on the most effective acts.

Tracking Progress:

Create a strategy to monitor your progress and assess the success of your career branding initiatives. Regularly compare your accomplishments to your predetermined goals and make any required adjustments. Celebrate accomplishments and milestones along the way to keep your professional branding journey inspiring and motivating.

"Elevate your career with a strong personal brand that reflects your authentic self and sets you apart in the professional world."

KEY TAKEAWAYS:

- Career branding is crucial in today's competitive job market to stand out and make a lasting impression.
- Understanding your brand involves identifying the unique qualities, values, and aspirations that set you apart.
- Building an impressive online presence, especially on platforms like LinkedIn, is essential to showcase your expertise and professionalism.
- Developing a strong professional reputation and credibility requires networking, obtaining testimonials, and continuously learning and growing.
- Soft skills, such as communication, emotional intelligence, and leadership, are fundamentals for success in any career.
- Effective presentation skills help you communicate ideas and make a lasting impression on your audience.
- Establishing content authority through valuable and well-researched content positions you as an industry expert.
- Adopting a growth mindset allows you to embrace challenges, seek feedback, and engage in lifelong learning for personal and professional development.
- Building a professional image involves paying attention to personal appearance, maintaining online etiquette, and aligning with industry standards.

Keep in mind that professional branding is a continual process that calls for constant work and reflection. Accept the trip, be flexible, and watch as your brand expands and thrives, creating doors to interesting new career prospects.

Chapter 7

HOW TO SUSTAIN YOUR SUCCESS?

Nurturing Success for the Long Haul

> *"Sustainable success demands continuous growth and adaptation in addition to initial milestones."*

True success goes beyond reaching an objective or level of accomplishment. It involves maintaining and expanding success along your chosen path, requiring dedication to flexibility, self-improvement, and resilience. In this chapter, we explore tactics and routines to navigate the dynamic world of success and ensure lasting accomplishments.

Success today is dynamic and ever-evolving. Consumer preferences change, industries face technological disruptions, and competition shifts constantly. To sustain success, staying current and adapting to change is crucial. Proactively understanding trends, staying informed about industry news, and connecting with innovation experts is iimportant. Embracing continual learning and adaptability fosters growth, thriving, and impactful contributions in your chosen field.

This chapter provides a range of tactics to help you build and maintain long-term success. By adopting these practices, you not only sustain your accomplishments but also continue to grow, thrive, and make a significant impact in your sector.

1: STAYING RELEVANT AND ADAPTING TO CHANGE:

> *"Victory comes to those who embrace change and adapt with the times."*

Being relevant in today's fast-paced environment is essential for long-term success. When it comes to remaining current and changing with the times, keep the following in mind:

Embrace Technology Advancements: Maintain up-to-date knowledge of pertinent hardware, software, and web resources in your industry. Investigate how these technologies can boost output and advance your abilities.

Monitor Market Trends: Keep a constant watch on changing consumer tastes, market trends, and industry developments. To foresee problems and spot growth possibilities, keep up with new product developments and innovations.

Engage in Continuous Learning: Attend conferences, webinars, workshops, and professional development activities as part of your commitment to lifelong learning. Examine certification programmes or focused training programmes that are in line with your goals.

Flexibility and Adaptability: Develop a mindset that is open to novel ideas, opposing perspectives, and innovative approaches. Accept change and push yourself. Being flexible is essential for continuing success.

Emphasise skills and competencies: Keep up with the talents that are in demand in your industry and work to continually enhance them. To maintain your value as a resource, look for possibilities for formal education, online training, and on-the-job training.

Keep in mind that maintaining your knowledge involves dedication, a proactive attitude, and continuing learning. You may continue to succeed and outperform your competitors in your field by embracing change, implementing new technologies, and coordinating with market trends.

2: CERTIFICATIONS:

"Certify your expertise to solidify your success."

A strong tool for validating your abilities and knowledge in a particular profession is certification. They act as concrete evidence of your knowledge, boosting your professional credibility and giving you an advantage over the competition.

Complement career objectives: Select certificates that are in line with your professional goals and the course you wish to take in your field. Do some research on the certification options and choose ones that are both well-recognised by specialists in your sector and related to it.

Known and Reputable Programmes: Choose credentials from credible, renowned programmes. Look for certificates that are respected in your sector and respected by both clients and employers. Because of their rigour and thoroughness, these certificates are more likely to be regarded and valued.

Commitment to Personal Growth: Your dedication to professional and personal development is demonstrated by your pursuit of certificates. It demonstrates your commitment to keeping abreast of business best practices and standards. Employees that make an investment in their development and take the initiative to learn new skills and knowledge are frequently valued by their employers.

Opportunities for Advancement: By earning certificates, you may be able to enhance your profession and find new opportunities. Professionals with certifications frequently have access to special employment options and are valued by employers. In a competitive employment market, certifications might give you an edge and even boost your income.

Keep in mind that certifications are lifelong accomplishments. For many credentials to remain valid, continual professional development is necessary. This stipulation guarantees that certified individuals remain knowledgeable about changing industry requirements and continue to be experts in their specialised domains.

3: ADVANCING EXPERTISE: FORMALLY / INFORMALLY ?

"Education is not a one-time event; it is a lifelong pursuit."

A key component of higher education is expanding one's horizons and deepening one's knowledge. By obtaining further degrees, such as a Master's or PhD, your access to leadership opportunities expand. But before beginning your higher education journey, it's important to consider below factors.

First thing First: You <u>don't need to leave your job & pursue the higher education</u>. Why because, the level of learning & exposure that we get in colleges / universities that's completely outdated. What you will learn there by investing lakhs of rupees & 2-3 years of your valuable time, would not help you much to grow your <u>in-trend knowledge base</u>.

Rather you can complete your Master's / Phd's with a distance learning program from a great university along with your job because that degree will be acting like an eligibility criteria to apply for leadership roles in various positions.

Specialised Knowledge: The possibility to acquire specialised knowledge in a particular topic is provided by higher education. A deeper comprehension of theories and concepts is provided coupled with improved analytical and critical thinking abilities. This knowledge can aid in career development and promotion.

Positions of Leadership: Your prospects of obtaining leadership jobs can be improved by advanced degrees. Higher degree holders frequently display intellectual rigour, problem-solving skills, and leadership potential that employers value. Such credentials may open the door to more responsible positions and roles at higher levels.

Alternative Routes: There are other paths to professional advancement without higher education. Alternative routes like industry certifications or specialised training programmes may give pertinent information and skills, depending on your industry and career ambitions. Think about if these options fit with your objectives and offer a useful, affordable way to obtain the required knowledge.

Cost-Benefit Evaluation Think about the costs associated with getting a higher degree. Examine the associated expenditures, including tuition, living expenses, and potential income loss during study periods (if you are leaving your job & then doing a higher degree). If you are just planning a higher degree for a salary hike, then you don't need it, rather you need a step by step guidance, what our community members from variety of backgrounds are getting & they are easily hitting 100% to 500% salary jump with just the preparation of 2-4 months.

> *"Keep in mind that continuous learning and being updated with industry advances are essential for remaining relevant in a changing professional landscape even after receiving a higher degree."*

4: INTERNAL GROWTH:

> *"The true measure of accomplishment goes beyond outward achievements and includes the inside transformation you experience."*

Achievements and external recognition hold significance, but long-term success primarily stems from personal and professional growth. To appreciate the importance of internal growth, consider the following essential factors:

Investigate Possibilities in Your Role: Seek for chances to grow your skill set and take on new tasks in your current role. Engage your boss in conversation and let them know you're interested in tasks or initiatives that will help you gain new knowledge and skills. Take charge of your career development by actively looking for advancement chances.

Cross-functional Assignments Volunteer: Participate in initiatives or projects as a volunteer to gain exposure to other departments within your company. This gives you the ability to learn more, work with colleagues from other backgrounds, and comprehend how various departments and roles interact with one another better. Your skill set can be expanded by cross-functional experiences, which will also increase your capacity to make a valuable contribution to the organisation.

Be open to continuing your professional development: Participate initerestingly in continuous professional development programmes. To keep up with the newest trends, industry best practices, and cutting-edge technologies, attend workshops, webinars, and industry conferences. These gatherings expose you to fresh viewpoints and great networking chances.

Look for coaching and mentoring: Seek for mentors or coaches who can offer direction, encouragement, and insightful advice based on their experiences. A mentor can be within your same organisation or outside it. He/She can help you with career obstacles and opportunities by providing guidance and information. Your personal and professional progress can be facilitated by coaching, which can help you pinpoint your areas of strength and weakness and create winning tactics.

By actively seeking out possibilities for advancement within your existing work, you not only acquire new skills and competencies but also show a dedication to ongoing improvement and personal progress.

5: ESTABLISHING A GROWTH MINDSET:

| *"Believe in your ability to grow, and success will follow."*

For continued success, a growth mentality must be established. It is the idea that with commitment, effort, and a positive outlook, you can increase your skills and intelligence. Examine the following important ideas when developing a growth mindset:

Accept Challenges: People who have a growth mentality see obstacles as chances to improve and learn. They welcome challenging assignments as opportunities to learn new skills and increase their capacities rather than avoiding them. Positively accepting obstacles enables both professional and personal progress.

Recognise Failure as a Learning Opportunity: Failure and setbacks are inevitable on the path to achievement. Individuals with a growth mentality do not consider failures to be permanent or indicative of their ability. Rather, they view failures as instructive experiences that offer new perspectives and guidance for growth. They improve their strategies after making mistakes, keep going despite setbacks, and learn from their missteps.

Be Constantly Improving: A growth mentality entails a dedication to ongoing development. It entails proactively seeking out feedback and being receptive to helpful criticism. People that have a growth mentality aren't embarrassed to ask for assistance, work with others, or pick someone's brain. They actively look for chances to advance their skills and flourish.

Limiting Beliefs Reframed: Face your self-imposed limitations and boundaries. Understand that skills may be acquired via effort, practice, and persistence. Instead of thinking "I can't," try thinking "I can learn" and "I can get better." Develop an enthusiastic and upbeat outlook that promotes personal development.

Emphasise Process and Effort: Place more emphasis on the effort and the process than just the result. Improvement and constant work are what lead to success rather than instantaneous achievement. Celebrate the accomplishments made along the way while acknowledging that learning and progress are ongoing processes.

Encourage Risk Taking: People who have a growth mentality are prepared to venture outside of their comfort zones and take measured risks. They are aware that learning and growth only happen when they push themselves past what is comfortable and familiar. Accepting risk-taking opens up new chances, experiences, and potential for personal growth.

A growth mindset encourages resilience, adaptation, and ongoing learning. You may rise above difficulties, take lessons from mistakes, and seize chances for both professional and personal development.

6: GIVING BACK AND MAKING A DIFFERENCE:

"True success lies not only in what you achieve but in the positive impact you make on others and the world."

Sustaining success depends heavily on giving back and making a difference. Evaluate the following important factors while deciding how to contribute to the larger good:

Determine Your Causes and Values: Consider the social or environmental issues that you find important. Choose the causes that are consistent with your morals and views.

Spend Time and Skills in Volunteering: Look for chances to donate your time and skills. Local projects, community centres, and nonprofit organisations frequently look for knowledgeable volunteers who can share their knowledge and experience.

Perform Community Service: Take part in community service projects and programmes that cater to the needs of your neighbourhood. This could be coordinating food drives, taking part in cleanup efforts, or giving support to neighbourhood schools and community centres.

Supporting and Mentoring Others: Discuss your expertise and experiences with aspiring industry professionals. Mentorship programmes offer advice and assistance to people just starting their careers.

Financial Support for Causes: Think about making a financial contribution to groups and causes that share your values. This could be giving money, supporting fundraisers, or sponsoring events.

"You may improve the lives of others and advance society by giving back and making a difference. Let your success serve as a motivator for progress."

7: STAY HEALTHY AND FIT:

"Achieve, Energize, Prevail: Empowering Yourself through a Healthy Lifestyle"

Maintaining good health is vital for sustained success. Prioritize self-care by adopting healthy lifestyle habits. Regular physical exercise improves cardiovascular health, boosts energy levels, and enhances cognitive function. Find activities that you enjoy and make exercise a regular part of your routine. Alongside exercise, pay attention to your nutrition. Eat a balanced diet that provides essential nutrients and fuels your body and brain. Ensure you get enough sleep to allow for proper rest and rejuvenation.

Additionally, manage stress effectively by incorporating relaxation techniques, such as meditation or deep breathing exercises, into your daily routine. Recognize the importance of mental well-being and prioritize activities that promote stress reduction and mental clarity. By taking care of your physical and mental well-being, you increase your productivity, creativity, and resilience.

> *"Remember, success is not just about professional achievements but also about leading a fulfilling and balanced life"*

8: MANAGE YOUR FOCUS EFFECTIVELY

"While many believe that time is the ultimate asset, but it is the power of focus that truly holds the greatest value."

Success is often associated with the belief that time is our most valuable asset. This is partially true, but it's crucial to understand that attention is just as important if not more so. No matter how much time we devote, getting the required results can be difficult if we lack sufficient attention. The efficacy of focus comes in its capacity to accurately direct our resources and energies towards our objectives. It makes it possible for us to organise our workload, get rid of interruptions, and spend our time well.

"We can maximize productivity and complete our goals if we focus on what is most important."

9: MAINTAINING MOMENTUM:

"Consistent Progress is the ultimate key to exponential growth."

It is critical to keep up the momentum and resist becoming complacent if success is to be sustained over the long run. When it comes to keeping momentum, keep the following things in mind:

Make New Objectives: Set new objectives to keep pushing yourself. These objectives need to motivate you and force you out of your comfort zone. Divide them up into more manageable goals so that you can feel progress and success along the way.

Regular Progress Evaluation: Regularly evaluate your development and make the required corrections. This is assessing how well you're doing, determining where you need to improve, and putting methods in place to get around barriers. Keep your approach malleable and fluid, keeping in mind that change is inevitable and may call for course corrections.

Recognise Achievements: Your accomplishments—large and small—deserve to be celebrated. Give yourself some credit for all of your efforts and successes. Celebrating accomplishments raises spirits and inspires continued progress.

Take Part in Continuous Learning: Continue your education and look for new opportunities. Keep an open mind and a curious mind, and constantly seek out ways to broaden your knowledge and skill set. Attend workshops, seminars, and conferences that are pertinent to your area of expertise to keep current on market trends and advancements.

Create a Supportive Network Around You: Create a network of mentors, friends, and coworkers around you who will inspire and motivate you to keep moving forward. Find those who can help you along the way by sharing your goal and offering insightful advice.

Observe and learn: Give yourself some time to consider your accomplishments and setbacks. Use your experiences as a way to grow by taking what you've learned from them. Accept feedback and make good use of it to raise your performance and judgement.

Adopt a Growth mentality: Develop a growth mentality that places a high priority on ongoing development. Accept the notion that success is a journey rather than a destination. Put more emphasis on the growth and development process as opposed to just the results. Accept challenges, keep going despite obstacles, and see failures as important teaching moments.

Commitment to Excellence: Strive for superiority in whatever you do. Deliver your finest work every time and strive for quality. To distinguish yourself from the competition, consistently surpass expectations and go above and beyond.

You guarantee ongoing success by keeping up the momentum, adopting a growth mentality, and pledging to continual progress. Keep in mind that success is a lifelong path characterised by tenacity, expansion, and quality.

"The true measure of success lies in its enduring impact on oneself and others."

KEY TAKEAWAYS:

- Take advantage of technological breakthroughs, keep an eye on market trends, practise continuous learning, stay current with industry news, and collaborate and network to stay relevant in a quick-paced setting.

- Obtain certificates to prove your knowledge, boost your professional credibility, and obtain an edge over the competition.

- To develop your career, gain access to leadership positions, and obtain specialised expertise, think about pursuing further education.

- Find ways to advance in your current position, take on cross-functional tasks, continue your professional development, look for coaching and mentoring, and be open to criticism to advance both personally and professionally.

- To support personal growth and achievement, embrace obstacles, see failure as a teaching opportunity, concentrate on continuous progress, reframe limiting beliefs, place an emphasis on the process and effort, and encourage risk-taking.

- Decide your causes and principles, support social or environmental concerns, and have a beneficial influence on others and the planet.

> **"By putting these key ideas into practice, you can ensure your success over the long term, stay flexible, relevant and have a positive impact on the world."**

Chapter 8

7 HIGH INCOME SKILLS [MUST LEARN ALONG WITH YOUR 9 TO 5]

Multiply your growth by accelerating your learnings.

> *"Your ability to explore the world outside your immediate circumstances will help you grow more than your surroundings ever could."*

In today's world, many working professionals find themselves confined to the traditional 9-to-5 routine. However, the true essence of success lies beyond the boundaries of a mere paycheck. It is in exploring additional avenues alongside your job. The year is 2023, an era defined by digital innovation, and while the opportunities are abundant, it ultimately boils down to your dedication and action.

Prepare to embark on a transformative chapter that will broaden your horizons and propel your growth. Within these pages, we will delve into indispensable aspects and skills that should not be overlooked while pursuing your career. Relying solely on a single source of income is no longer prudent in your journey. Keeping your options open is paramount, as the future remains uncertain, and unexpected possibilities may arise.

Let's tap into the zone of endless possibilities!

1: THE FREEDOM TO FLOURISH: BOOST YOUR POTENTIAL AS A FREELANCER:

> *"Harness your skills, embrace flexibility, and embark on an independent journey where success knows no bounds."*

In the world of freelancing, autonomy and adaptability is king. There are various advantages of working as a freelancer, such as project choice, remote work, enhanced pay, wide career possibilities & much more.

Basic steps to kickstart freelancing:

Selecting a Niche: When choosing a niche/topic, it's essential to find a specialised area within the industry that suits your abilities / hobbies / experience and aligns with market needs. To carve out your distinct niche, thoroughly explore the top trending areas on various gig platforms.

Building a Powerful Portfolio: Make a client-centric portfolio to attract customers that showcase your Talent. Display your best work, references, and experiences. Make use of online networks and platforms to increase visibility. Provide good valuable service to get repeat work & referrals.

"Freelancing is the best & easiest form to start multiplying your growth along with your regular job and it <u>doesn't comes under Dual Employment</u> because you are not working under the pay-roll of two different companies as their official employee. Rather, here you are working with different clients, that too in your free time after office hours."

2: PUBLIC SPEAKING: SECOND BIGGEST FEAR AMONGST HUMANS

Public speaking is a word that can cause more fear in humans than in the name of death. Today's people are afraid to express themselves adequately. Fear of judgement, guilt of stumbling while speaking. People think Public speaking is only for extroverts, those whose mouths never shut, but is it really the truth?

No, it's just a myth. Public Speaking is for all and it is a learnable skill. Public speaking is for all those who have ideas in their mind and are ready to express but only fear of judgement is holding them back.

It is an integral part of communication in an organisation. One should learn the skill of public speaking for a smooth and clear flow of communication with teammates and colleagues. But how would you learn public speaking?

Well, start with the basics.
- Start by talking to yourself in the mirror. You are not afraid of speaking. You are afraid of speaking in front of a person. Chase that fear by speaking with yourself in front of the mirror. Let words catch your mind, let ideas flow like a breeze, and talk without fear with yourself.
- You can also explore joining a Toastmasters club nearby, where you can attend trial sessions for free. This will give you a platform to practise and gain confidence while speaking in front of an audience.

Resultantly as your start getting better at it, then you can explore public speaking assignments in various settings, such as colleges, schools, coaching institutes, and small organisations. These opportunities allow you to speak on different topics and engage with students

As you progress further, You can start taking sessions in corporations for professionals on technical or non technical topics for one to three hours per session. By participating in these speaking engagements, you can enhance your public speaking skills and professional growth too. These public speaking stages not only will boost confidence but also will add as a source of income for you. So, Public speaking skill won't only help you as a skill in your career but you can monetize that skill by conducting fruitful sessions.

"So, Remember Public speaking is not just about what you say but how you say it."

3: PROJECT MANAGEMENT: TRANSFORMING CAREERS, UNDERSTANDING LEADERSHIP

"Create your own route to success by honing your abilities, strategizing, and taking opportunities."

Learning and honing specific talents all over time is required for career advancement. Years of experience alone do not guarantee immediate promotion to project lead or manager. You may notice that certain people in your firm or project reach these positions early in their careers. This is because they actively practised the appropriate actions and tactics long before you were aware of them. To position yourself for early professional advancement, you must consider numerous angles and dimensions while actively developing the following skills:

Taking Care of Work Responsibilities: Take charge of your responsibilities and offer high-quality results on a regular basis. Set an example by being dependable, finishing projects on time, and exceeding expectations.

Being an Effective Team Player: Effectively collaborate with coworkers, speak honestly, and actively contribute to team goals. Maintain a good attitude, help others, and promote a collaborative work environment.

Managing Difficult Clients: Learn how to handle difficult client relationships while remaining professional, moderating expectations, and finding win-win solutions. Develop strong interpersonal skills to properly handle stressful situations.

Having Clear and Bold Communication: Confidently and assertively express your thoughts and ideas. Proactively share your point of view, raise issues, and seek clarification as needed. Leadership requires effective communication skills.

Contributing with a Sense of Duty: Take the initiative and show a proactive attitude. Look for ways to contribute outside of your current function, to give new ideas, and to recommend improvements to processes and workflows.

Participating in Project Refinement: Take part in the process of enhancing projects every step of the way. Demonstrate your eagerness to learn from mistakes, adapt to changing conditions, and contribute to project enhancements. Seek feedback and engage actively in project reviews and lessons learned meetings.

4: SALES AND NEGOTIATION: LEVERAGING THE POWER OF VALUE-BASED SELLING:

"Value-Based Selling: Where Service and Success Align"

The most widespread **misperception** about sales is that, it is entirely about making money. On the other hand, true salesmanship goes far beyond transactions and includes the skill of giving outstanding service and effectively articulating the value of what you have to offer. It's about realising that **selling is serving**.

The goal is to communicate and market the inherent worth of your products or services. By emphasising the benefits and distinct advantages they offer, you create a compelling case that goes beyond features and price points. When the value proposition you give, outweighs the cost, you create a perfect scenario for both yourself and the buyer, in which the trade is not only rational but also ethical.

Considering the reference of our training community, which is always welcoming new members. The benefit people gain from membership is far more valuable than the financial investment they commit. The real benefits they receive, such as knowledge, resources, assistance, results, far outweigh the fractional amount they pay. Our community ensures that the value delivered greatly overpowers the financial commitment necessary by striking this balance.

This value-based selling notion extends beyond sales contexts. When negotiating a job offer, for example, the ctc package you get should be considered appropriate if the value you bring to the organisation exceeds the monetary figure you propose. By highlighting your abilities, expertise, and future contributions, you establish a convincing argument that justifies the company's investment in recruiting you.

As a result, it is critical to <u>hone your sales and negotiation skills</u> while embracing the underlying principle of value. By doing so, you empower yourself to take ownership of your professional journey, express your authority, and navigate mutually beneficial outcomes. You can open new prospects, create solid relationships, and achieve incredible success in your sales and negotiation endeavours if you focus on giving outstanding value.

"Your Sales & Negotiation skills will help you in every aspect of your journey."

5: FACING THE CAMERA: THE MOST TRENDING SKILL OF THIS DECADE

Video making is becoming a necessity for every working individual.

But why is this happening? Why video making is required? Why do we need this kind of art?

You may be aroused with these kinds of questions. See, It's not about the personal preferences but about embracing today's digital platform.

Let me share a simple yet impactful example. <u>Video resumes</u> have entirely changed the game on job search platforms like Naukri and LinkedIn. When applicants go beyond the standard (paper resumes) and show themselves in short <u>60-90 second video resume</u>, their profiles shoots up to the top 2% of candidates. This shows that video-making allows you to express yourself, showcase your personality, and makes you stand out from rest of the world.

The significance of video-making goes far beyond mere job applications. It strengthens you in countless ways. As you dive deeper into video creation, you'll notice a remarkable improvement in your confidence levels. Your language skills will improve, and you can talk more easily. With video making, you can share your ideas and knowledge from the comfort of your home with people worldwide, not just in your city or country. The world is evolving & you also need to adapt it now.

Let me tell you something personal, my life got completely changed by the power of making videos. Back in **2019**, when i started practicing this art, in just <u>seven months, I created over 550+ videos</u> and their impact on my life is beyond my wildest imagination.

I became completely different, discovering new facets of myself through making and sharing videos. These videos have become life lessons. I now have the privilege of imparting my thoughts, ideas, knowledge to thousands of people every month. It's an incredible transformation that wouldn't have been possible without embracing the skill of video making.

So, making videos can be used in a lot of ways. It can change your life, go beyond what you thought was possible, and take you to places you never thought you could go. Enjoy this art form, utilise its magic, and unlock opportunities.

"Together, let's build a future where creating videos becomes not just a skill but a way of sharing ourselves and making a good impact on the lives of others."

6: COPYWRITING: ADDS MAGIC TO YOUR CONTENT BY INVOKING EMOTIONS & CURIOUSITY

Copywriting isn't just another skill; it's one thing that every worker should learn. Your best skills come down to how you show your information, craft your words, and hook your readers. It's all about giving your viewers an experience, getting them excited, and making them want more.

This is one of the TOP PAID SKILLS across the world.

Copywriting skills are important if you want to send a message that really sticks with your readers. It's not just about putting words together; it's about telling a story that makes people feel something and gives the impression that you know what you're talking about. With the right words, you can build trust, create a sense of urgency, and get people to act. This skill of yours can make all the difference in your emails, messages, proposals & much more.

It's is an art that requires you to know the power of words and how to use them successfully. It's about coming up with interesting stories, catchy headlines, and convincing calls to action. Every line you write should have meaning, every paragraph should make the readers feel something, and every piece of material should have an effect that lasts.

Don't forget that Copywriting isn't just about writing. It's also about connecting, persuading, and getting people to act. It's a skill that will help you get ahead in your career and make you stand out. Use the power of persuasion in your writing, and make sure that your words leave a permanent impact on everyone who reads them.

7: THE POWER OF GUIDANCE: NURTURING YOUR POTENTIAL THROUGH MENTORSHIP:

"Learn from the wise, embrace guidance, and accelerate your growth through the wisdom of experienced mentors."

In a mentoring relationship, a more seasoned mentor imparts information and skills to a less seasoned mentee. The mentor serves as a teacher, offering guidance, inspiration, and helpful criticism as the mentee actively absorbs and develops from their knowledge.

Benefits of Mentorship:

- **Accelerated Learning:** Mentorship allows us to gain insights and wisdom that would take years to acquire independently. Mentors help us avoid pitfalls, make better decisions, and develop skills faster.

- **Expanded Perspectives:** Mentors offer fresh perspectives on goals, challenges, and opportunities. They provide insights we might overlook and challenge limiting beliefs, broadening our horizons and enabling informed choices.

- **Networking and Connections:** Mentors have extensive networks in their fields, granting us access to valuable contacts, collaborators, and career opportunities. They can introduce us to key individuals and help establish meaningful relationships.
- **Personal Development:** Mentorship promotes personal as well as occupational growth. Mentors function as role models, instilling virtues such as strength and honesty in their students. They offer suggestions for work-life balance, challenges, and emotional intelligence.

Finding the Right Mentor:

- **Self-Analysis:** Reflect on goals, aspirations, and areas needing guidance to find a mentor whose expertise aligns with your needs, ambitions & purpose.
- **Seeking Resonance:** Look for a mentor with common values, mutual respect, and good chemistry. Trust and effective communication are crucial for a strong mentor-mentee relationship. In short, just think, are you able to resonate with the person on a deeper level?
- **Implementor** - Accelerate your progress and effectively implement your goals by tapping into the knowledge and insights of seasoned professionals who have already achieved what you are striving for.

Cultivating an Effective Mentorship:

- **Clear Expectations:** Establish clear goals and communicate your focus and desired outcomes. Ensure alignment between mentor and mentee.

- **Active Engagement:** Engage with your mentor by seeking guidance, asking questions, and sharing progress. Take responsibility for your growth and invest in the relationship.
- **Gratitude and Reciprocity:** Show appreciation for your mentor's time and wisdom. Consider ways to give back and recognize their contributions. Mentorship is a two-way street.

Mentorship multiplies growth by providing guidance, support, and insights from experienced individuals. It accelerates learning, expands perspectives, and opens doors to new opportunities.

"Have a mentor in your life as well as have a mindset of being a mentor in someone's life too"

KEY TAKEAWAYS:

- Unlock your potential by choosing a specialized niche and building a client-centric portfolio. Embrace the freedom, flexibility, and limitless possibilities of freelancing.

- Take charge of your responsibilities, be an effective team player, manage difficult clients, communicate clearly, and actively contribute to project refinement to accelerate career advancement.

- Focus on delivering value beyond transactions, emphasize the benefits of your products or services, and develop strong sales and negotiation skills.

- Seek mentors aligned with your goals, benefit from their insights, actively engage with them, and show gratitude and reciprocity.

- Hone your skills with time such as Video Making, Copywriting, Public Speaking.

> **"Accelerate your growth by embracing freelancing, project mismanagement, value-based selling, mentorship, and public speaking."**

Chapter 9

5X YOUR PRODUCTIVITY

Turbo-charge Your Productivity & Potential with Strategies, Tools, and Habits for Success.

> *"Productivity is not just about getting more done; it's about achieving what truly matters."*

The ability to be extra-efficient has become essential for success in today's fast-paced world. Achieving what matters the most is more important than simply completing more tasks. It's crucial for establishing a healthy work-life balance and achieving your goals, whether you're a professional, an entrepreneur, or a student.

We'll also cover few powerful productivity tools that can revolutionise the way you work by facilitating seamless performance, efficient task completion, and superior organisational skills. You may revolutionise the way you work, streamline your processes, and strengthen teamwork to increase productivity by implementing these techniques and tools into your daily routine.

Come, let's dig deeper!

1: PRACTICE DIGITAL DETOX TO SPICE-UP YOUR PRODUCTIVITY.

> *"Unplug to get Recharged"*

Constant media connectivity can hinder productivity by leading to distractions and information overload. The idea of a digital detox will be discussed in the following section, along with practical tips for occasionally unplugging from technology.

Getting through distractions: The modern world is awash with emails, social media updates, notifications, and unending streams of information. Your attention is diverted by these distractions, which makes it harder for you to concentrate on challenging tasks. You can reclaim control of your attention and focus on the task at hand by keeping your digital devices away from you for 1-2 hrs to complete your priorities in a distraction-free environment.

Setting limits: Engaging in a digital detox means placing limits on how much time you spend on technology. Establish dedicated device-free areas and times of the day when you avoid being distracted by technology. This deliberate disconnection from technology frees you up to do other things, like spend time with loved ones, pursue hobbies, or just take alone moments to think creatively.

Screen Free Ritual: Your productivity can significantly increase if you include screen-free rituals in your daily schedule. Spend time without any digital gadgets doing things like writing, meditation, tactile reading, and nature hikes. These practices offer a mental reset, lowering tension and anxiety while fostering a more relaxed and concentrated mental state.

> *"Witness the dramatic benefits, a digital detox may have on your productivity and performance."*

2: DELEGATE TASKS TO TEAM MEMBERS WHEN APPROPRIATE.

Delegation is an instrument for maximising productivity, encouraging teamwork, and promoting success as a whole.

Giving tasks to others is not a sign of weakness but rather a calculated decision that will increase productivity. Efficiency can be greatly improved by delegating responsibilities to your team members in an optimum manner.

Choose the right tasks: Not all tasks can be assigned to others. Understand which tasks can be completed by others while ensuring that they are compatible with their skills and availability. Concentrate on assigning activities that require a lot of time or are outside of your area of expertise.

Choose the right candidates: Select team members who possess the abilities and expertise required to complete the assigned tasks. To make sure they can accept more duties without feeling overburdened, take into account their workload and availability.

Clearly define your expectations: The objectives, timeframes, and any special instructions or restrictions related to the assignment should all be made clear. To prevent confusion or delays, make sure that everyone on your team is aware of what is expected of them.

Give assistance and resources: Set your team up for success by giving them the materials, information, and tools they require to successfully execute the assigned tasks. Provide direction and remain accessible for inquiries or further explanations as necessary.

Trust and empower your team: Delegation is more than just assigning duties; it is also about allowing your team members to take ownership and make decisions. Trust their skills and give them the freedom to complete the work in their way so that they can feel ownership and accountability.

> *"When you delegate, you create time for yourself to focus on what truly matters."*

3: FOCUS ON ONE TASK AT A TIME, MULTITASKING IS A MYTH.

"Quality and efficiency thrive in single-tasking."

Contrary to popular beliefs about multi-tasking, what I feel is multitasking often leads to decreased productivity and diminished quality of work. Single-tasking is beneficial for quality, effectiveness & creative output because of undivided attention on a particular task.

Deep focus: Concentrating on a single thing without interruptions enables you to fully immerse yourself, which improves comprehension and problem-solving.

Effective task completion: Multitasking may appear to increase productivity, but it causes you to work more slowly. You can work more effectively by avoiding time-wasting context switching and concentrating on one activity until it is finished.

Fewer errors: Dividing attention & focus among different tasks increases the chance of errors. You can retain precision and attention to detail by committing yourself to one work at a time.

Improved execution of tasks: Single-tasking promotes efficient prioritisation and time management. The Pomodoro Technique and other scheduling strategies can increase productivity and improve the ability to prioritise. You can greatly enhance your workload management skills by adopting these techniques and concentrating on one activity at a time.

"Accepting one task at a time will help you focus deeply, complete tasks quickly, and manage your time more effectively."

4: LEARN TO SAY NO AND AVOID OVERLOADING YOUR SCHEDULE.

"Saying no to the unnecessary, opens doors to the extraordinary."

Spreading yourself too thin and taking on too much can hurt your efficiency. Maintaining a healthy work-life balance requires the ability to say no politely.

Creating boundaries: By refusing, you can set up distinct boundaries and safeguard your time and energy. Recognising your limitations and effectively conveying them can help you avoid piling up duties that don't support your priorities or your objectives.

Examining requests and opportunities: When presented with fresh requests or chances, take the time to assess how well they fit into your current workload and goals. Think about how embracing them would affect your timetable and general output. Prioritise opportunities that are consistent with your values and objectives and decline them with grace.

Declining politely: Saying no doesn't have to be confrontational or negative. You can gently and respectfully deny. While expressing your gratitude for the chance, be sure to mention that you are currently unable to accept any more commitments. Provide alternatives, such as naming a different person who might be able to help or urging a future partnership.

"You can avoid overwhelm, give priority to important things, and create a successful and rewarding career."

5: UTILIZE PRODUCTIVITY TOOLS.

"Work smarter, not harder, with the right tools in hand."

In today's digital era, a plethora of productivity tools are available to streamline workflows and enhance efficiency. By embracing the right tools, you'll harness technology to boost your productivity.

ProofHub: A comprehensive project and task management tool that centralizes activities, projects, and communication. It offers features like Gantt charts, time tracking, and file sharing, promoting productive communication, effective task management, and streamlined project workflows.

Calendly: Simplifies scheduling meetings by allowing you to personalize meeting links, set availability preferences, and share them with others. Participants can easily book conversations with you based on both of your availabilities, eliminating the need for back-and-forth email exchanges and saving valuable time.

Todoist: A powerful task management program that helps you stay focused and organized. You can create tasks, set due dates, and priorities, and collaborate with others on shared projects. With features like reminders, repeating tasks, and project templates, Todoist ensures that you efficiently manage your tasks and nothing slips through the cracks.

Notion: A versatile note-taking and information management tool that offers a user-friendly and adaptable workspace. You can customize your notes, interact with team members, and create structured databases. Notion improves productivity by providing a centralized platform for capturing, organizing, and retrieving information.

Hive: An efficient project management platform that integrates work management, collaboration, and real-time communication. With features like customized project views, visual Kanban boards, and integration with popular technologies like Slack and Google Drive, Hive enables seamless collaboration, project progress tracking, and streamlined workflows.

By utilizing these productivity tools, you can optimize your workflow, enhance collaboration, and achieve greater productivity. These tools empower you to work smarter, not harder, by leveraging technology to streamline tasks and focus on meaningful work.

6: SET REMINDERS OR ALARMS TO STAY ON TRACK.

"Stay on top of your game with timely reminders."

It's simple to lose track of deadlines and tasks in our fast-paced world. Alarms and reminders can help with that. Why they are essential for productivity is as follows:

Effective scheduling and organisation: Reminders serve as valuable tools for maintaining organization and preventing oversight. To effectively manage your time, establish reminders for important deadlines, meetings, and milestones, enabling you to stay on track and meet your objectives.

Proactive Task Management: Add due dates and tasks to Google/ Apple calendars in your devices. These Reminders alert you when something needs your attention, avoiding last-minute scrambles and assisting you in finishing activities on schedule.

Flexibility and Adaptability: Tailor reminders to your preferences. Pick from physical alarms, digital calendars, or smartphone apps. Create customised frequency, sound, and visual cues to increase productivity.

Utilise the power of alarms and reminders to stay focused, organised, and productive. Take a proactive stance, and you'll notice a difference in your productivity and job output.

7: KEEP A CLEAN AND ORGANIZED WORKSPACE.

"A tidy space fuels a focused mind."

The environment in which you work has a significant impact on your productivity. A neat desk promotes concentration and productivity. Distractions and diminished concentration might result from a cluttered and disorderly atmosphere.

Distractions should be kept to a minimum: Keeping your workstation tidy lowers visible and mental distractions, allowing you to focus on your activities.

Boost productivity: A well-organized workspace helps you discover what you're looking for fast, saving you time so you can spend more of it working.

Improve focus: Having a neat workspace encourages mental clarity and keeps you interested in your work, which improves concentration and produces higher-quality work.

Enhance ergonomics: Take into account the ergonomics of your workspace to provide comfort and reduce physical discomfort that could interfere with your productivity.

You may encourage productivity by setting up a tidy and organised workspace. Create efficient filing systems, purge your physical and digital spaces of clutter, and organise your workspace. Enjoy the advantages of a concentrated and effective workplace.

8: PRIORITIZE TASKS, FOCUSING ON IMPORTANT ONES FIRST.

"Focus on the vital few, not the trivial many."

A productive workflow must be maintained by effective prioritisation. You can move significantly closer to your objectives by concentrating on the tasks that matter.

Make the distinction between important and urgent: Not every assignment is made equally. The capacity to differentiate between urgent chores that require immediate attention and significant actions that advance long-term objectives is necessary for prioritisation. You may avoid getting sucked into a never-ending loop of busy work and make sure that your efforts are in line with your goals by concentrating on what matters most.

Use tested frameworks: There are many frameworks available to assist you in effectively prioritising. Examples, include the Pareto Principle, the ABC approach, and the Eisenhower Matrix. These tools offer clarity, allowing you to group jobs according to their urgency and importance.

Allocate time and effort wisely: Once you've established your priorities, allocate your time and effort accordingly. Set aside specific times for crucial tasks and shield them from interruptions and distractions. Avoid switching from one task to another without finishing the previous one.

> *"You may improve the clarity and direction of your work by becoming an expert at **prioritisation**. You choose wisely where to spend your time and effort, ensuring that you go forward with the projects that matter."*

9: REWARD YOURSELF AND GAMIFY YOUR WORK SCHEDULE.

> *"Make productivity a game, and success becomes your reward."*

Productivity can be increased by incorporating incentives and rewards into your daily tasks. You can make work enjoyable and keep motivated by making activities feel like a game.

Motivation and engagement: Gamifying your work schedule, adds excitement and challenge. To stay motivated, set attainable goals, monitor your progress, and employ small-small rewards that motivate you.

The feeling of accomplishment: Approaching work like a game helps tasks and milestones feel like accomplishments. Reward yourself for your continuing productivity and sense of fulfilment by acknowledging your progress.

Enhanced concentration and dedication: Games cultivate heightened concentration and unwavering dedication. By establishing a system that encourages progression, games nurture resilience and enduring perseverance

"You may foster a healthy work atmosphere by making productivity a game and rewarding yourself for reaching milestones. Accept gamification to boost output and have fun on the path."

10: DEFEATING PROCRASTINATION: UNLEASH YOUR PRODUCTIVITY POTENTIAL

Procrastination, a common obstacle that hinders productivity and delays important tasks, can be overcome. It often stems from factors like fear, lack of motivation, or feeling overwhelmed. However, by understanding the psychology behind procrastination and implementing effective solutions, you can break free from this barrier and re-discover your full potential.

Increasing Motivation: Explore various strategies to spark inspiration and overcome the sluggishness of procrastination. Start by clearly defining your goals, envisioning the desired outcomes. This approach enables you to gain momentum and propel yourself towards taking action.

Chunking Tasks: Divide complex or daunting tasks into smaller, more manageable chunks. This method makes the tasks less overwhelming and allows you to experience a sense of progress and success by focusing on one small step at a time, which in turn motivates you to keep moving forward.

Accountability and Support: Foster accountability by sharing your objectives and progress with others. Consider finding an accountability partner or joining a group of like-minded individuals who can provide support and encouragement. By externalizing your commitments, you enhance your sense of responsibility and dedication to overcoming procrastination. *For reference,* when the working professionals get inside our training program for hiking their salaries, they are put into a zone of all like minded folks, who are working towards a similar goal. *I truly belive that "*<u>your environment is stronger than your will power</u>*" and if you are surrounded with right people, procrastination will not be surrounding you. :) :)*

11: MAINTAIN SUSTAINABLE PRODUCTIVITY HABITS.

"It is not just about short-term bursts of high output—it's about maintaining consistent performance over time."

Energy management: Make the most of energy levels by determining peak times and scheduling tasks accordingly. To maintain high-quality work, take pauses, exercise, and participate in energising activities.

Work-Rest Rhythms: Maintain a balance between work and rest to increase productivity. Utilise planned breaks to refresh your thoughts and keep your clarity and attention.

Self-Care: Prioritize self-care through a healthy lifestyle, sufficient sleep, mindfulness, and positive relationships. Improve resilience, reduce stress, and boost productivity in the long run.

Boundary Setting: Establish clear work-life boundaries. To guarantee undisrupted focus and personal time, establish specific work hours and clarify expectations.

Create long-lasting productivity habits to set yourself up for long-term success. Set boundaries, work-rest cycles, self-care, and energy management as top priorities. Keep in mind that sustained production is a marathon that demands self-care and reliability.

"Harness the Power of Productivity: Unlock Your Full Potential and Accomplish Remarkable Results."

KEY TAKEAWAYS:

- Delegate tasks for increased productivity, utilizing others' skills while focusing on priorities.
- Prioritize effectively to concentrate on impactful tasks, avoiding trivial ones.
- Take breaks from technology, reduce distractions, and gain fresh perspectives.
- Polite refusal and setting boundaries prioritize tasks and prevent overwhelm.
- Utilize productivity tools for streamlined workflows and efficiency.
- Reminders keep you organized, manage time, and adapt to your preferences.
- Maintain a tidy workspace for improved focus and productivity.
- Single-task for deep focus, fewer errors, and better time management.
- Incentives and rewards make work enjoyable and increase motivation.
- Allocate dedicated time blocks for tasks, maintain focus and improve time management.
- Master time management for the organization, meeting deadlines, and maximizing time.

By implementing these key strategies, tools, and habits into your daily routine, you can unleash your productivity potential and achieve what truly matters.

Chapter 10

STORIES OF TRANSFORMATION (ACHIEVERS)

Bringing Out the Extraordinary: Transformational Journeys

> *"Your way towards exceptional career begins when you have faith in the remarkable possibilities hidden beneath commonplace circumstances."*

As we approach the final chapter of this book, let us take a moment to reflect on the incredible journey we have embarked on together. Over the course of the previous nine chapters, we delved deep into the techniques that have revolutionized the professional lives of countless individuals, enabling them to recognize their true worth. This transformative experience has been characterized by profound insights, game-changing tactics, and a guiding light that has inspired us all.

Within the Massive Hike Formula community, (online + offline) workshops and training modules led by Saurav Pal have been instrumental in equipping everyone with the necessary tools to open up their full potential. These transformative teachings offer a comprehensive roadmap for attaining career success, financial advancement, and personal fulfilment. Individuals within the community have gained the skills required to overcome challenges, navigate career transitions, and secure their dream jobs. Through the collective sharing of knowledge and proven tactics, the community has empowered each other to flourish in their professional journeys.

In this concluding chapter, we will explore the experiences / journey of those who have gone through the unconventional paths in their lives. There are **thousands of success stories & achievers inside the community**, hence it was very difficult to choose just 7 out of them. Still we have handpicked few amazing transformation journeys for you. As you read, you will find common ground with their struggles and path, with which you will be able to resonate with.

Ms Priyanka Sharma

https://www.linkedin.com/in/ml-developer/

Got 3 Big Hits in 3 consecutive years [2020, 2021, 2022] despite the pandemic

"Elevating Professional Career, Achieving Unprecedented Success"

Hi, I'm Priyanka Sharma, an IT professional with over 4 years of experience working in an MNC. I specialise in Cloud Data Engineering and have also worked in the field of data science. Initially, I found myself assigned to Mainframe technology, which didn't align with my interests. I needed to select the right technology to enjoy my work and advance in my career. That's when I met Saurav in 2019, who became my mentor and provided valuable guidance in choosing the right path and securing a decent hike.

Before joining the Massive Hike program in August 2020, I faced several hurdles in my career journey. Within my organisation, I struggled to find fulfilling projects as I was randomly assigned to Mainframe technology, which was not my area of interest. I was unsure of how to transition to a different technology that suited me best, feeling confused and dissatisfied with my career.

However, my encounter with Saurav, who had faced similar challenges in his journey, really inspired me. Learning about his (Massive Hike Formula) Program and witnessing his commitment to helping others, I became an enrolled member, joining a group of like-minded individuals. Looking back, I consider this investment as one of the best decisions I've ever made.

Since joining the highly accountable group, I've achieved remarkable results in terms of salary hikes and CTC growth. <u>My salary has increased by over 400%</u>, rising from **3.78 LPA to 20 LPA**. Throughout my 3 year career span across three organizations, I witnessed significant progress, starting from 3.78 L and reaching

6 L in my second organization. Then finally moved to 20 L in my next role.

Top 3 learnings that changed my life:

<u>First</u>, working in the right direction and choosing the ideal technology can lead to desired results in terms of domain knowledge, CTC, and overall success.

<u>Second</u>, having the right mentor and being part of a community of like-minded individuals instead of trying alone.

<u>Third</u>, identifying and working on our weaknesses consistently can foster our personal and professional development.

In terms of interviews, I have participated in over 30, and I have received 15+ offer letters. By implementing the tricks, techniques, and steps learned from Saurav's <u>Hikers Community</u>, I attracted numerous interview opportunities and surpassed my expectations with the number of offers received.

I take immense pride in sharing this, that me & my brother were able to **gift a car to my family**. Additionally, I provided more substantial financial support & paid off loans and all the credits. I achieved the dream of pursuing an MTech in Data Science, which was made possible due to increased savings and financial stability.

Without a doubt, the best investment I have made so far is in getting touch with Saurav & his training program. Joining the community exposed me to invaluable knowledge, introduced me to like-minded individuals, and allowed me to grow under his guidance, resulting in tangible results and returns.

A Note from Saurav:

"Priyanka is the first member of our enrolled community group, even still she is using the learnings & group environment to uplift her career regularly. I am so proud, how she is growing & making her family's dream into reality."

Ms Sowjanya

https://www.linkedin.com/in/soujanyatech/

366% Pay raise despite 50 months of Career Gap

"Defying Limits: Consistent Progress is the only way"

I'm Sowjanya, a professional in the fields of L&D and Project Management. With over 4 years of experience as an LMS administrator and project handler, I excel in utilizing various LMS tools like SAP SuccessFactors, Cornerstone on Demand, Saba Cloud, Moodle, Canvas, and Veeva CRM. My expertise lies in implementing projects, planning strategies, and managing data migrations.

Despite the numerous challenges in my previous roles, career gap & much more, I never gave up. My determination paid off as I achieved significant results in terms of my career growth. I got the highest offer of **366% Hike** but I chose to join another company that gave me 200% jump due to location constraint.

As my financial stability increased, so did my confidence in myself and my abilities. However, I also learned that money alone does not guarantee happiness. Nevertheless, I now enjoy a more comfortable lifestyle compared to before.

What Pushed me in this Journey?

As a woman, I aspired for financial independence and equal earning opportunities. My desire for personal growth, a comfortable lifestyle, and peaceful nights of sleep fueled my determination.

Despite a career gap of more than 50 months, I managed to secure a job and reach a leadership position within just 4 years. Gave more interviews, Optimised my profile on all platforms, made video resume, rigorous followup techniques, systematic reach out on linkedin & much more things that I was asked to do with the guided mentorship of Saurav & his team.

With my time management skills, I am balancing my job responsibilities along with family commitments. I am very happy & excited to share that I made significant investment moves, utilised my major earnings/savings as a **down payment to purchase a house**. Looking ahead, I plan to explore real estate investment opportunities.

Once I became part of the community, I shifted from a negative to a positive outlook, gained higher levels of confidence, and experienced a sense of happiness replacing my previous unhappiness, understood a lot of concepts that no-one told in my career life. Additionally, the sense of connection within the community <u>removed my feelings of loneliness</u>.

I believe my journey is a picture of resilience, determination, and unwavering pursuit of success. I hope my experiences inspire others facing similar challenges, illustrating the power of self-belief and continuous personal growth.

I always wanted to set up right examples & inspirations for other women in our society. We all have equal opportunities, don't restrict yourself.

Mr Justin Xavier

https://www.linkedin.com/in/justin4data/

500-600% Salary Jump is easily possible!

"Beating Challenges, Scaling CTC, and Embracing Infinite Potential"

The person who never backs down from a challenge is me, Justin Xavier. My career began as a Marine engineer, but I took a risk and changed to information technology, where I fell in love with data analysis. I started as an IT analyst, developed into a skilled data analyst, and now I want to rule the data science industry.

My ultimate objective is to enhance artificial intelligence by pushing the envelope. I receive the support and empowerment from the private group in various forms like the 1 CC Mastermind and Hikers + Scaling Batch, and I am appreciative to my mentor, Mr Saurav Pal, for his priceless counsel and direction.

In my Massive Hikers journey, my biggest challenge is to achieve the highest possible CTC. Things were not moving as per my plan, still I chose to remain optimistic about my future earning potential and I›m excited about the possibilities that lie ahead. My unwavering commitment and readiness to tackle challenges always proved to be the turning point.

Through the "Massive Hike Formula" trainings, I have achieved remarkable results in terms of CTC growth. The program has equipped me with strategies for peak performance during interviews, enhanced my technical skills, and empowered me to negotiate higher possible offers. With a well-thought-out long-notice period game plan, I can smoothly transition to my dream job, feeling confident and prepared.

Participating in the Hikers Program has provided me with invaluable learnings. I have discovered that a <u>500-600% salary hike</u> is not only possible but achievable, even in challenging times. The program has boosted my self-image, confidence, and conviction, which spills over into all areas of my life. I have also learned that fast-tracked appraisals are within reach through consistent value delivery and positive contributions to my organization.

To achieve my high CTC, I have planned to attend numerous interviews, armed with the skills and confidence gained from the program learnings. The modules focused on confidence boosting, high CTC negotiation tactics, bonuses beyond CTC, premium companies roadmap, massive hike scaling, and formula have prepared me to tackle the job market and receive more job offers, ultimately securing my dream job.

Now I am constantly exploring new technologies in data science and AI keeps me at the forefront of my field. My role as a father brings me immense joy and inspiration. Lastly, I am grateful for my loving and supportive wife, who shares my passion for excellence.

Joining the Massive Hike and 1 CC Mastermind Program has brought about positive mindset changes for me. I now feel confident in achieving a higher CTC, understand the importance of crafting my narrative, and realize the potential to build a successful income streams. The supportive community provides me with energy, motivation, and a shift towards abundance and possibility thinking. As a proud 1 CC Mastermind member, I experience success, empowerment, growth, mindset shifts, and unlimited potential, accelerating my progress.

Mr Naresh Kukkala

https://www.linkedin.com/in/naresh-kukkala/

55+ Interview attempts, 13+ Offer letters received

"Breaking Boundaries, Growing Success: Harnessing the Power of Massive Hike Formula"

I'm Naresh Kukkala, my journey started with setbacks and a lack of confidence during my school years, but I overcame those obstacles and pursued my passion for electronics. I completed college and obtained an M.Tech in Industrial Mathematics with Computer Application. My professional career began with an internship, and I gradually switched positions to build expertise and increase my earning potential. Currently I am working in iOS app development and am passionate for lifelong learning.

In 2021, while working for Infosys, I came across an advertisement for the Massive Hike webinar. Intrigued, I attended the webinar and discovered the "Massive Hike Formula" a detailed result oriented course by Saurav Pal. After careful consideration, I decided to join the program. Being a part of the Hikers community allowed me to identify my weaknesses, take necessary actions for improvement, and gain confidence. With a strategic 3 month notice_period, I planned my job switch, resigned without an offer letter, and started attending interviews.

Despite initial struggles, I persevered and received multiple offer letters. Eventually, I secured a job with a <u>remarkable 150% hike</u> on my existing CTC, going from **9 LPA to 22.5 LPA**. Alongside my career growth, I started teaching mobile app development and built a personal brand, attracting people organically who sought my guidance and expertise.

Throughout this journey, I learned valuable lessons. I recognized the importance of personal branding on professional platforms like LinkedIn to attract interview opportunities. Stepping out of my comfort zone and challenging myself led to personal and professional growth. Networking with like-minded individuals became integral to my success.

I also recognized the importance of having a side hustle along with my job. I started exploring opportunities like freelancing & what else can be done in my free time/weekends. Learning has no end.

My journey was fueled by the desire to challenge the industry standard salary hikes beyond the traditional 5-10% increments. I participated in approximately 55 interviews and successfully cleared 20 of them. **I received a total of 13 offer letters, with the first offer letter coming after 15 interview rejections**.

I am proud that I have been able to transform myself from an introvert to an extrovert through teaching, and also fulfilling my passion for bike rides and travel, particularly my memorable journey through Ladakh.

I would say, never loose hope. Your initial interview failures are eventually preparing you for the bigger success. Keep progressing & keep improving.

Mr Tejomay Saha

https://www.linkedin.com/in/tejomayonline/

Roller Coaster Ride from 14.5 Lakhs to 41 Lakhs

"The Hike Transformer: An Epic Journey from Doubt to Doubling Success"

As a skilled Technical Lead at 3Pillar Global with over 8 years of industry experience, I, Tejomay Saha, am passionate about tackling challenges and driving innovation in cloud-native backend solutions using AWS infrastructure.

During my journey I encountered several obstacles:

- Initially, I struggled to receive interview calls & scheduling interviews, and the few calls that I did receive were from relatively unknown startups.
- Negotiating for salaries was another big challenge.
- Handling long Notice Period, as recruiters were not agreeing to wait for me.

My impatience and tendency to overanalyze led to feelings of fear and doubt. I also held the belief that surpassing my current salary would not be possible for me. However, everything changed when I decided to join the Hikers (Formula + Scaling) program and started receiving incredible support from the community.

Saurav's mentorship proved game changer, I achieved significant results in my journey. Within just 3 months, I secured 10 offers from top multinational corporations and product-based companies. In total, I participated in over 90 interviews and cleared more than 35 technical rounds. My previous CTC was 14L at that time & I started receiving the offers with 20L, then 25L. I further got 27L, 30L, and 34L. And the happiest part is currently I am working on **41 Lakhs**(39.5 Fixed + 1.5 Variable).

The Hikers Program provided me with invaluable insights. I came to understand that mindset plays a crucial role, accounting for 80% of the impact in achieving massive results, while skills contribute the remaining 20%. By breaking through limiting beliefs and embracing the power of taking initiative and massive action, I unlocked my true potential. I also learned the importance of contributing to the community, helping others, and maintaining a positive mindset.

As I started earning more money, a sense of empowerment, confidence, and gratitude washed over me. I found fulfilment in supporting my family›s dreams and aspirations, and I began contributing more to charitable causes. With newfound financial stability, I embraced the concept of Financial Independence Retire Early (FIRE) and developed a mindset focused on creating a greater impact in the world.

Earlier I use to feel <u>undervalued and unappreciated in my previous roles/companies</u>. This pushed me to seek better opportunities where my contributions would be recognized. My journey not only led to career success but also left a purpose driven impact on my perspective.

Joining the Saurav's mass movement had a deep impact on my mindset. Witnessing the impressive results achieved by fellow hikers instilled hope and belief in my journey. Breaking through limiting beliefs, doubling my salary in just three months, discovering hidden potentials, and reigniting my childlike energy are just a few of the incredible changes I experienced.

I extend my heartfelt gratitude to my mentor Saurav and my family, who played instrumental roles in my success.

Ms Lekha Ravindran

https://www.linkedin.com/in/lekha-ravindran16/

Outstanding Achievement from 3.6L to 21 Lakhs even being on a higher experience & comfort zone.

"The Unstoppable Journey to a 500% Salary Increase: From Struggles to Soaring Heights"

Born in the Tirupathur district of Tamil Nadu (April 1991) and raised in Bangalore. Growing up in a large joint household, I faced numerous difficulties & failures. At the age of 10, I was diagnosed with a brain tumour, which led to academic struggles due to subsequent surgery and memory problems.

Despite these challenges and my fear of communicating in English, I remained determined to complete my school & college in 2012. Then I started working in the BPO industry at IBM, initially earning 7,000 monthly. Later, I switched jobs to Infosys, where I worked in the tech support domain with 16,000 salary.

In 2016, I joined a new company, continuing to gain work experience. However, I realized that my salary did not match my growing experience. Feeling demotivated, I questioned my abilities and feared changing jobs due to financial commitments.

But then in 2021, after struggling for 9 years in my career , something happened that changed my life upside down, when I came across Saurav Pal and his Massive Hike Formula (MHF) program. Despite the initial doubts, I decided to enrol, recognizing the need to break out of my comfort zone and overcome several hurdles in professional life. Joining the MHF community proved to be a BIG TURNING POINT for me. With the guidance and mentorship provided, I discovered a new sense of independence, happiness and became an inspiration to others both inside and outside the community.

Through my dedication and the timely guidance, I achieved an impressive 500% hike in my salary, reaching 21 Lakhs and also got promoted to become a Project Manager.

Throughout my Massive Hike journey, I encountered various hurdles. Overcoming my fear of change and lack of confidence were significant obstacles I had to face. Additionally, I faced challenges in profile building, interview confidence, Hr Convincing, that I eventually conquered with the help of the MHF community.

My mindset underwent a significant transformation. I developed the courage to face interviews and interact with new people, and I learned to step out of my comfort zone. I now embrace failure as a learning opportunity and strive to inspire and motivate others.

Earning a higher salary brought me a sense of financial freedom and the ability to clear my loans and EMIs quickly. I began to understand the difference between working for money and making money work for me.

WHY I kept moving throughout my Massive Hike journey, was to challenge my own limiting beliefs. I questioned my fears, the negative thoughts holding me back, and the reason for failure. By breaking free from my comfort zone, I embarked on a transformational journey and inspired others.

Also, I stayed focused on personal development and honing my skills. I realized that to excel in my career, I needed to enhance my knowledge and stay updated with the latest industry trends. I actively sought out opportunities for professional growth, attending webinars, workshops, and industry conferences.

One area I prioritized was improving my communication skills. Recognizing that effective communication was crucial in my role as a Project Manager, I joined Toastmasters. Through consistent practice and dedication, I gained confidence in my ability to articulate my thoughts clearly and engage with others.

Throughout my Massive Hike journey, I remained grateful for the support and encouragement I received from my family, friends, and the MHF community. I learned the importance of surrounding myself with like-minded individuals who shared my aspirations and pushed me to achieve my goals.

My transformation was not limited to my professional life. As I grew personally and financially, I also became more involved in social causes. I actively participated in community service activities, volunteering my time and resources to make a positive impact on society.

I truly feel, this life is meant to achieve big and that can only happen when we take right actions.

Mr Nikhil Bhole

https://www.linkedin.com/in/nikhil53/

Reached nearly 40L with just 3+ Yrs of Experience [Bahrain, UAE]

"From CAT Failures to Overseas Placement"

Bhusawal, a town in northern Maharashtra, is where I was born and raised. There, I lived for the first 17 years of my life. I decided to become an electrical engineer in 2018 to pass the CAT exam. But from 2017 to 2020, I had four back to back CAT failures.

I lost all hopes to prosper in my career & then during this time, I started attending live online events & sessions. I came across an advertisement for the «Massive Hike Formula» program. I registered for the workshop and enrolled in the Massive Hike Formula (MHF). With live sessions of Saurav, I started expanding my knowledge. I heard professionals sharing their journeys of achieving 200%-250% salary hikes. It really gave me a ray of hope.

There were few fellow members in MHF program who achieved early results with 70%-80% salary hikes within <u>just 10 days</u>, while for me it took a while to prepare my authoritative CV, video resume, Naukri profile, and LinkedIn profile. When I scheduled my first interview, I was rejected within 4 minutes after being asked a few technical questions.

But I didn't give up & kept giving interviews with progressive preparation and improvisations. However **after my 30th interview, I received my first offer letter, with (100% Jump)**. Despite the offer, I wasn›t confident enough to resign immediately due to the misconception that a higher salary meant more responsibility. I remember discussing this with Saurav, who told me, «The higher you move in the hierarchy, the less (ground level work) you›ll do.» I started applying the learnings from Massive Hike Formula & Scaling both.

In the initial phase of my journey, <u>I followed a few strict rules</u>:

- Contact and discuss deeper topics with those who appeared live in the community sessions.
- Never miss any Massive Hike Formula or Massive Hike Scaling sessions.
- Quickly plan and take action on what I learned in the discussion. In case of procrastination, I would take a single day off and complete all pending actions on that day.

The Massive Hike Scaling strategies brought me amazing opportunities with offers of 11 LPA, 14.2 LPA, and 17.2 LPA (Delloitte). Finally, I resigned with a 317% Hike offer letter in my hand. Interestingly, during my notice period, about 60% of my team also resigned and moved to product-based banking. Hence, I received easy referrals for all the banking giants, including Goldman Sachs, Morgan Stanley, JP Morgan Chase & Co., and Credit Suisse. However, I failed to secure offers from any of them.

Along with learning from the online training modules of saurav, I also attended his physical event (Hikers Retreat 2022). The impact of that live transformative experience was so significant that <u>I gave over 35 interviews within three weeks immediately after the retreat event</u>.

I received an offer of <u>25 LPA</u> from Airtel (Gurgaon). And a few weeks later, I received a **much bigger offer from Bahrain (UAE)**. At that point, I had no prior knowledge about Bahrain, so I researched the place, including the cost of living, culture, and food, within two days and initiated the exit process.

Two notable aspects that helped me during this transition were:

- Shrinking my notice period from 60 days to under 20 days.
- Grabbing a handsome joining bonus over the offered Overseas package.

<u>In March 2023, I arrived in Bahrain</u>, and by applying Saurav›s guidelines in my daily work, I can see positive results even in my current company. Some memorable moments include attending the Massive Hikers Retreat 2022, watching live sessions from my Bahrain office, and experiencing the vibes of working Abroad.

CONCLUSION

So as you finish this chapter, think about the opportunities that are still open to you. Take advantage of focussed communities & groups where you network with like minded people and expand your opportunities. The insights that is offered throughout this book is for your transformational journey. Your route to a rewarding and fulfilling profession is here.

Remember that you can maximise your potential to crazy heights and forge a future that exceeds your expectations. The success stories of those who have gone before you on this path serve as evidence that extraordinary changes are not only feasible but also within your reach.

Wishing you success, happiness, and unshakeable faith on yourself. It›s time to live a grand life. The world is eagerly awaiting your triumph.

Our book comes to an end here, but your transformation journey has to begin from here and I along with my entire team is there to help / support & guide you.

"Self-discovery, resiliency, and unshakable belief are lifelong journeys. Embrace it because you can uncover a future beyond your wildest fantasies."

The End

Kickstart your learning & Implementation:

https://www.sauravpal.com